Coal Towns in the Cascades

COAL TOWNS
in the
CASCADES

A Centennial History of
Roslyn and Cle Elum, Washington

John C. Shideler

Second Edition

Futurepast
Arlington, Virginia

Futurepast: Inc.
2111 Wilson Boulevard, Suite 700
Arlington, VA 22201
www.futurepast.com

Library of Congress Control Number: 2005909208

ISBN 0-9710464-4-1

Printed in the United States of America
06 07 08 09 10   10 9 8 7 6 5 4 3 2 1

First edition © 1986 by Melior Publications

∞ The paper used in this publication meets the minimum requirements of the American National Standard for Information Sciences—Permanence of Paper for Printed Library Materials, ANSI Z39.48-1992.

*To the present and future residents
of Roslyn and Cle Elum*

Contents

1. The Primeval Environment 1
2. The Conquest of Native Peoples.............11
3. The Pioneer Era 27
4. Railroad! 39
5. Immigrant Stew 57
6. Mining King Coal.................................77
7. Logging in Kittitas County 91
8. Coal's Struggle for Survival...................101
9. The End of an Era................................125
10. Shaping the Future..............................137

Notes 147
Acknowledgments 149
Author's Note on Sources...........................150
About the Author and the Second Edition..151
Index 153

CHAPTER 1

The Primeval Environment

For all but a few descendants of pioneers, the events that shaped the upper Kittitas Valley before 1886 may seem to belong to a timeless period of prehistory. From the visual evidence of civilization, the area's history may appear to begin only with the discovery of coal, the building of the railroad, or the opening of logging camps. But the history of Roslyn and Cle Elum would be far different had nature not preceded the handiwork of man with her own majestic sculpting of the physical environment of the upper valley. The geological and biological processes that formed the region have a history that dates back hundreds of millions of years. A century ago citizens of the United States came to this land and within a few decades began to alter what nature took millions of years to create. How this beautiful and richly endowed environment evolved serves as the point of departure for the history of Roslyn and Cle Elum.

Washington's Geological Landscape

Geologists recently have developed new theories that explain the origins of the Cascade Mountains and other major features of the Washington landscape. These theories derive from a better understanding of the movement of floating plates that comprise major portions of the earth's outer crust. This process is known as "continental drift" or "plate tectonics." It is particularly important for understanding the origins of Washington, because the state is located at the edge of the North American continental plate.[1]

More than two hundred million years ago, the western edge of the North American plate traced a line that today follows roughly the boundary between Idaho and Washington. The continent met the Pacific Ocean here, and no dry land existed immediately to the west. But events in the Atlantic Ocean initiated change: as that plate began to grow, North America moved west, with important consequences for the Pacific Ocean plate.

This is Cape Disappointment, near mouth of the Columbia River (on facing page).
Photograph courtesy of the Northwest Collection, Spokane Public Library.

This drawing explains what happens when two continental plates collide: the heavier one sinks beneath the lighter one at a "subduction zone."
Diagram by David Alt and Donald Hyndman, reprinted by permission of Mountain Press, Missoula, Montana.

The Old Coastal Plain

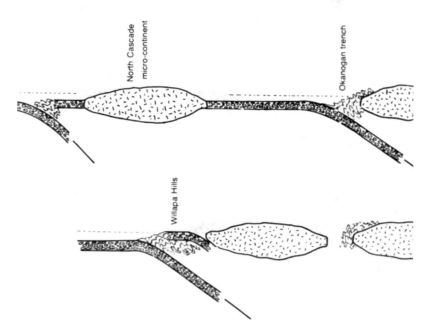

A plate tectonic scenario hypothesizes the docking of the North Cascade microcontinent against western North America.
Diagram by David Alt and Donald Hyndman, reprinted by permission of Mountain Press, Missoula, Montana.

Such fossil palms grew in Washington approximately fifty million years ago.
Photograph courtesy of the Burke Museum, University of Washington.

As North America inched westward, the denser Pacific Ocean plate slipped under the continental plate. In this subduction zone a kind of trench was created where the greatest amount of surface friction occurred. Below, the surface rock that once lined the ocean floor underwent intense heating. The Rocky Mountains resulted when granitic magma from below the earth's surface cooled, crystallized, and became uplifted. The mountains' rise was linked to the closing of a trench and the docking of a new land mass on the continent's western edge.

The North American continent and Pacific Ocean plate moved slowly but steadily over millions of years. Smaller land masses were also adrift. In the relatively short space of fifty million years, two of these collided with North America to give the state of Washington much of its present size and shape. According to recent theory, the coal fields of Washington began as long ago as a hundred million years as coastal swamp lands on a mountainous island adrift in the Pacific Ocean. These swamps and marshes straddled a "North Cascade microcontinent" that was advancing inches per year toward a collision with North America. When that happened some fifty million years ago, the subcontinent crunched its eastern edge up

against the continental plate of North America. Thus ended the island's long migration from somewhere in the southwest Pacific Ocean to the northwest American coast.

Cle Elum and Roslyn are situated near the southeastern limit of the exposed portion of this subcontinent, while the coal fields from Centralia to Issaquah define a southwestern edge. Many millions of years ago, a wet and gentle coastal climate fostered the luxuriant growth of plants on both coasts. Then, as plants died and fell to the ground, marshy land developed which the passage of time converted into peat bogs. Sand and other sediments separated successive layers of plant material, forming the geological strata that over millions of years were compressed into layers of coal and sandstone.

The "docking North Cascades microcontinent" theory accounts for certain differences that have been noticed among fossil specimens of animal life in the North Cascades and close relatives of similar animal groups in areas farther to the east. Many animal fossil remains resemble far more closely animals of the same age found in Southeast Asia than those found in the Okanogan highlands and Rocky Mountain regions. In the area around Cle Elum, the absence of dry land animal fossils supports the theory of prior coastal conditions.

More support for the idea that the North Cascades microcontinent approached Washington from the southwest is derived from the orientation of rivers and valleys in the central and northern Cascades. These almost invariably trend northwest, a direction that suggests the application of force from the southwest. Such a force would have been exerted as the microcontinent docked against the former coastline of the North American plate approximately fifty million years ago.

The arrival of the North Cascades microcontinent furnished Washington state with the second of two major building blocks. Earlier, perhaps as long as one hundred million years ago, the southern edge of a smaller Okanogan microcontinent had docked against the continental edge of North America in what is now northeastern Washington. This accretion left a vast ocean bay in the Columbia Basin area of Washington and in northeastern Oregon.

After the North Cascades microcontinent closed that area in, volcanoes in the basin became active and flooded eastern Washington and Oregon with thousands of feet of volcanic rock known as basalt. The lava flows from these sources traveled as far west as Lookout Mountain, just east of Cle Elum. This ridge is composed of basalt from lava flows that filled a former river valley and then eroded less rapidly than the surrounding rock.

The causes of the volcanic activity in the

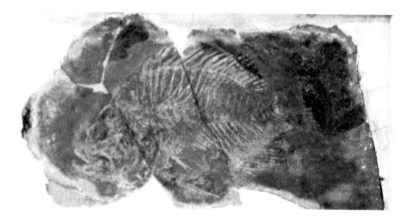

Columbia Basin area are not well understood, because these volcanoes became active about twenty-five million years after the North Cascade microcontinent docked onto the North American continental plate. Perhaps there was a link between the commencement of activity in the Columbia Basin and the extinction of volcanoes in the Cascades at that time. The Cascade range volcanoes reignited later, of course, as subterranean rock liquefied about fifty miles inland from the zone of subduction off the Washington coast. This process has continued to the present day with the slow swallowing of eastward moving portions of the Pacific Ocean plate.

Some important geological events that affected coal mining in Cle Elum and Roslyn occurred during the Eocene epoch (fifty-five to forty million years ago). During the early Eocene, the North Cascades microcontinent ended its transoceanic voyage to North America. When it arrived, its coastal areas were flat, but the force of the crush against the existing land mass folded the coal bearing strata and inclined them at an angle to the surface. This is known to have occurred during the middle Eocene, because lava from volcanoes in the Cascades that erupted in the later Eocene (approximately forty million years ago) exhibit far less folding than the coal beds.

The movement of continental plates, the

This fossilized fish swam in the shallow waters of Kittitas County during the Eocene epoch.
Photograph courtesy of the Burke Museum, University of Washington.

docking of islands, and the uplifting of filling material from closed trenches or subduction zones provide the dramatic backdrop to the formation of Washington's geological landscape. But these geological processes did not complete nature's canvas, whose texture and tones evolved through continual erosion and uplifting for many more millions of years.

Washington's climate has varied dramatically during the last sixteen million years. It has ranged from wet and tropical during the late Miocene epoch (thirteen to sixteen million years ago), to a dry climate during the Pliocene epoch (two to ten million years ago), to an unstable and variable climate in the Pleistocene, the geological epoch that ended with the last ice age about ten thousand years ago. The vary-

This fossil preserves deciduous leaves from the Paleocene or Eocene epochs.
Photograph courtesy of the Burke Museum, University of Washington.

This fossilized fern is an example of lush plant life that once grew in abundance in Kittitas County.
Photograph courtesy of the Burke Museum, University of Washington.

ing climates have produced different types of weather that affected patterns of plant and animal life as well as the pace and the extent of surface erosion.

During the Eocene epoch, Washington's climate was warm and moist. Dinosaurs inhabited North America and plants flourished. Across Washington state a subtropical climate encouraged the growth of giant palm fronds, forests of broad-leafed and conifer trees, and innumerable vines and shrubs. The local climate was favorable to vegetation in part because of higher concentrations of carbon dioxide that existed in the earth's atmosphere. According to recent research, the level of carbon dioxide in the air is related to the rate of continental drift and volcanic activity. Following is a description of how these geochemical processes that recycle carbon work:

"When rain clouds pile up in the sky, carbon dioxide from the atmosphere dissolves in the water droplets and forms a weak acid. The slightly acidic rainwater falls on continental rock and percolates through the soil, picking up still more carbon released by the roots of plants. In the process of weathering, water also collects calcium and other dissolved minerals from the soil. When the runoff reaches the sea, minute organisms called plankton use the carbon combined with calcium to form shells. As these creatures die, their calcium carbonate shells collect in shallow regions of the sea floor to form limestone. At a subduction zone, where the ocean floor is gradually sinking beneath a continental plate, limestone is carried deep into the Earth's interior.

"At the high temperatures inside the Earth, carbon dioxide is then driven out of the limestone and eventually winds up in the molten roots of a volcano. Carbon dioxide reenters the atmosphere when a surface volcano erupts or when an undersea volcano sends it bubbling back into the ocean, where it reaches the air from the water's surface and the cycle begins again. For eons, through the influence of this global movement of carbon, the Earth has maintained a climate hospitable to life."[2]

Particularly significant for the history of Roslyn and Cle Elum is the discovery that the concentration of carbon in the atmosphere has varied from one period to another throughout the earth's history. Without periods of high concentration, far less carbon would have been available to nourish the plants that provided the raw material for Roslyn's coal. But during the warm and moist periods of the dinosaur age, thick layers of plant matter accumulated. Regularly these were covered by meandering rivers that formed ponds and deposited sands and gravels. In time the weight of sediment compressed sand into sandstone and decomposed vegetable matter into first peat then coal.

A six-inch pen at the upper right indicates the scale of this fossilized "Sabalites palmetto."
Photograph courtesy of the Burke Museum, University of Washington.

Scientists theorize that fifty to one hundred million years ago the earth's continental plates moved faster, and that increased subduction of carbon-laden ocean crust and heightened volcanic activity caused a greater proportion of the earth's stock of carbon to be released into the atmosphere as carbon dioxide. This produced a "greenhouse effect" and higher temperatures during the coal forming period. During the succeeding geological epochs, the amount of carbon dioxide in the atmosphere declined, affecting both plant life and the climate.

The contrast is most dramatic during the Ice Age that visited the earth from six hundred thousand to as recently as ten thousand years ago. According to recent investigation of "fossil air" from polar ice packs, the amount of carbon dioxide present during the Ice Age was as little as two-thirds the amount that existed at the beginning of the industrial revolution around 1800. The cause for such a reduction is uncertain, but the effects are well known: a general atmospheric cooling and the formation of huge glaciers covering as much as two-thirds of the earth's surface.

The Ice Age of the Pleistocene epoch was of signal importance to the Pacific Northwest. During four separate periods lasting from fifty to one hundred ten thousand years each, glaciers scoured mountain peaks and valleys. Thus, the sharper relief of the high Cascades results in large measure from the effects of glaciation. But beyond their contributions to sculpting landscapes, the Ice Age also provided a landbridge across the Bering Strait that enabled migrating Asians to find their way to the Western Hemisphere some seventeen to twenty thousand years ago.

America's First Immigrants

It took a global cooling of the earth to transfer water from the ocean to the North American glacier, laying bare a path from Asia to Alaska. With global temperatures averaging some ten to twelve degrees Celsius lower than at present, glaciers absorbed sufficient water to lower ocean levels by more than 350 feet. For a time, glacier free western Alaska became an extension of Asia occupied both by animal herds and the people who pursued them. For several thousand years, man and beast alike were corralled behind an impenetrable glacier that blocked access to south central Alaska and to the warmer regions of North America that lay to the south.

During this period, from approximately 17,000 years B.P. (before present) to approximately 12,000 years B.P., the Asiatic peoples of Alaska depended upon their control of fire and mastery of hunting, fishing, and sewing skills to provide food and protection against cold nights and winters. In time the hardy bands of people who met the challenge of nature increased both their skills and their numbers, especially as the earth again entered a warming phase and the land around them became greener and more

A Native Explains Creation

The Indian People, recognized as the Fourteen Tribes under the Treaty of 1855 and known as the Yakima Indian Nation, do not believe that their ancestors came across a "land bridge," but that they are bound by the Laws proclaimed to them by the Creator. These laws are pronounced solidly in the Yakima Washut faith which is also known as the Seven Drum religion. The Laws, in the form of songs, were delivered to the Indian People upon their placement on the earth during the separation of the land forms of the world during the last destructive force, the Flood. The Washut songs are the Indians' Bible. They tell of what was, what presently is taking place and what is to come in the final destruction.
—Cecelia Eli (Yakima)

hospitable. Gradually the glacial barrier receded, finally opening a corridor just east of the Canadian Rockies through hundreds of miles of remaining ice.

A stream of wildlife and people surged through this gap approximately twelve thousand years ago, opening most of the western hemisphere to human occupation. Some of the first of these immigrants settled in the Pacific Northwest. Others moved on to more southern climes in the present United States, Mexico, and Central and South America. For a thousand years these new Americans pursued abundant wildlife, until populations dwindled or became exhausted. Such species as the mammoth and the mastodon were probably hunted to extinction, as were horses. Gradually, the many native groups adapted to changing

Cecilia Smith Ashue with a berry crop at Potato Hill on the Yakima reservation.
Photograph courtesy of the Yakima Nation Library.

conditions. Some evolved complex societies and civilizations, sustained by farming and animal husbandry. Others reacted to depleted resources by fanning out over larger territories. Still others diversified their food supplies and learned to live in greater equilibrium with nature's bounty. The natives of the Pacific Northwest adjusted to their environment. They learned to live from hunting, fishing, and the gathering of edible plants.

As a gateway to the American continents, the Pacific Northwest was among the first regions outside Alaska to be settled by humans. Corroboration of this theory has come from archaeologists who excavated the Marmes rockshelter along the Palouse River in southeastern Washington. It dates from approximately 10,000 years B.P. and provides the earliest evidence of human occupation ever found in the Americas. Further confirmation has come from the Olympic Peninsula in western Washington where the death of a mastodon that lived 12,000 years ago was linked by archaeologists to evidence in the skeletal remains of the perhaps lethal projectile point.

The Northwest's Earliest Inhabitants

The Pacific Northwest's earliest human inhabitants probably missed the catastrophic effects of the final "Spokane flood" of the last Ice Age. This deluge was caused by the breaking of the ice dam that contained a huge glacial "Lake Missoula" in western Montana approximately sixteen thousand years ago. Its release was responsible for the present appearance of the channelled scablands in eastern Washington and the final scouring of the several sets of coulees,

or river courses, that cut through the topography of eastern Washington.

The same warming trend that occasioned the last Spokane flood cleared the ice from a corridor through the Canadian glacier and opened the Western Hemisphere to human settlement. The effects of the global warming were probably barely perceptible to early residents of the Pacific Northwest. In the Northwest, the study of twelve-thousand-year-old seeds has revealed that Washington's climate was much cooler than at present, with brief and moderate summers—much like those found today in northern subarctic climes.

Changes brought about by man probably influenced the composition of wildlife resources more rapidly than did the effects of the earth's gradual warming. Although some biologists believe that large animals like mammoths, mastodons, and bison were better suited to the cool, moist, and monotonous climatic conditions of the recent Ice Age, it is almost certain that the extinction of these species was accelerated if not entirely caused by human predation. In any event, native populations in the Northwest have long practiced hunting. Projectile points as old as twelve thousand years have been found, and a device for throwing spears or darts known as an *atlatl* was developed at least by 8,500 B.P. But the earliest evidence for the bow and arrow, a more powerful hunting weapon, dates only from

A Yakima Indian in ceremonial dress pauses in front of a teepee.
Photograph courtesy of the Yakima Nation Library.

it was composed of several groups that wintered at Union Gap and also at locations farther north, such as at Lake Cle Elum. Well before historic times the Yakimas had abandoned the rockshelters, caves, and pithouses of early native groups for tule mat long houses, and occasionally for the teepees and log structures that were common to natives of the American plains and western Washington, respectively. The villages of the Kittitas–Cle Elum group were located along the Yakima River near Thrall, Ellensburg, and Thorp, and in the upper valley near the confluences of the Swauk and the Teanaway rivers. For centuries before the arrival of Europeans, the Yakimas maintained a stable existence in natural harmony with the resources of nature.

3,500 B.P.

Anthropologists believe that the early Americans inhabiting Washington balanced their diets by eating meat, fish, and roots, berries, and greens. The organization of life in native communities probably focused upon cycles of hunting, fishing, and gathering, but it would be erroneous to assume that life was an unremitting struggle for survival. If modern aboriginal societies are any guide, the search for food could have occupied as little as two or three days per week for most families. This left sufficient time for the performance of ceremonies, the playing of games, and the development of cultural and economic relations between native groups of differing regions.

The tribe that in modern times is known as the Yakimas lived in the valley of the Yakima River from its confluence with the Columbia to its headwaters near Snoqualmie Pass. The name Yakima signifies "people of the gap or narrow waters," and

Tule mat long houses, like this one at Priest Rapids, was typical of Yakima family dwellings.
Photograph courtesy of the Yakima Nation Library.
Photograph by C. Relander.

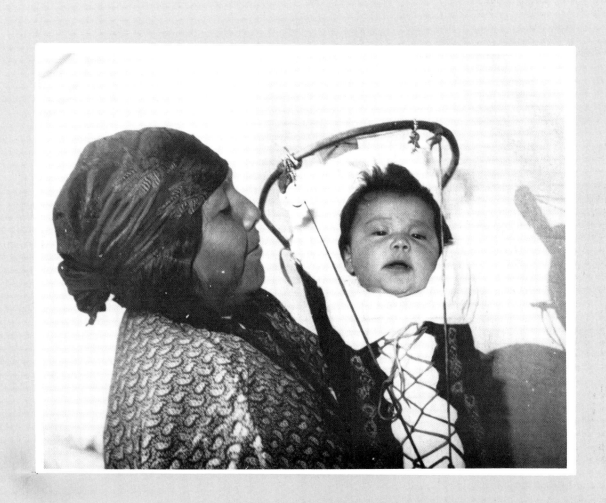

CHAPTER 2

The Conquest of Native Peoples

Before contact with whites, native Americans enjoyed a comfortable existence in the area that is now Washington state. West of the Cascades, the rivers and estuaries that drained into Puget Sound and the Pacific Ocean supported the largest concentration of aboriginal peoples anywhere north of Mexico. East of the mountains, tribes such as the Yakimas roamed over a larger territory than their western neighbors, but still found fish and game in plenty, and harvested roots and berries. A limited commerce and shared religious perspectives stimulated a generally peaceful coexistence among Northwest tribes.

The common bond among Washington tribes is exemplified in a Chinook creation legend set at Lake Cle Elum. In this story, the wise Coyote grappled with a monster beaver named Wishpoosh who drowned and ate all the people who tried to fish there. During their struggle the great beaver's dam broke, causing a great flood that carved many of the geological features of eastern Washington and the Columbia Gorge. The battle between Coyote and

Wishpoosh raged all the way to the Pacific Ocean, with neither able to gain the upper hand.

Finally Coyote changed himself into a tree branch and Wishpoosh foolishly swallowed him. Inside the beaver's stomach, Coyote used his stone knife to cut Wishpoosh's sinews. The beaver died, and Coyote and Muskrat took its body to shore. There they cut apart the beaver and threw its parts far and wide.

"The head became the Nez Perce, great in council. The arms became the Cayuse, powerful with bow and warclub. From the legs came the Klickitats, famous runners. From the ribs came the brave Yakima. From the belly came the Chinooks and coast tribes, the short people with big stomachs. At last Coyote had only the hair and blood. This he flung far to the east, where it became the Snake and Blackfeet and Sioux, the tribes of war and blood. Then the Coyote said, 'The Earth is full of inhabitants, there is no longer place for me.' And he ascended into the sky."[1]

The Yakimas and other Washington tribes preserved their independence and ways of life longer than many other native peoples. As early as the days of Christopher Columbus, North American natives had suffered at the hands of European conquerors, traders, and explorers. The pattern was set at the time when imperial Spain fueled its period of European prosperity with the easy plunder of Aztec riches from Mexico. Although some natives might have wished that pale skinned conquerors would liberate them from yokes of indigenous servitude, this notion was quickly dismissed. And, where native Americans were not suffering under self-imposed domination, as in Mexico, the idea of sharing native lands and resources with Spanish armies and landlords had even less appeal. As a consequence, European domination and colonization more often than not were established by the force of arms and by the equally deadly spread of fatal diseases among the natives.

In North America, the Spanish worked the greatest destruction on native American populations during the sixteenth century. The discovery by Balboa in 1513 of the Isthmus of Panama enabled Spanish conquistadores to build ships in the Pacific and to master the west coasts of the American continents. The Aztec civilization in Mexico fell to Hernan Cortes in 1521, and other conquests followed throughout the century. All were accompanied by great loss of human life, with some estimates placing the reduction in native populations after the first one hundred years as high as ninety percent.

Spanish explorers soon sailed north from Mexico along the Pacific coast. Bartolome Ferrelo reached the forty-fourth parallel in Oregon as early as 1542, and in the decades that followed Spanish sea captains established trading relations with Indian tribes as far north as Alaska. By 1730 the Yakimas had acquired horses from Spanish dominions, though it was not until 1767 that Spain finally established a military government in California. By this time Russia's political and commercial control over Alaska and its trading activities as far south as San

This drawing of a vessel under sail standing in the mouth of the Columbia River is by Woodfield.
Photograph courtesy of the Northwest Collection, Spokane Public Library.

The Northwest America was the first vessel built on the Northwest Pacific coast.
Photograph courtesy of the Northwest Collection, Spokane Public Library. Engraving in the Lenox Library, New York, by R. Pollard from a drawing by C. Metz.

Francisco created a barrier to Spanish expansion in the Northwest.

From the European perspective, Spanish explorers contributed significantly to increased understanding of Northwest geography. This is amply evidenced by the number of Spanish place-names associated with the inland waters and islands of northwest Washington. While probing Northwest waters, the Spanish developed commercial relations with Indians. The Spanish Captain Juan Perez visited Nootka Sound on Vancouver Island in 1774, and found the natives interested in iron for implements. But not all captains had successful experiences. In 1775 Bruno de Hezeta and his ship the *Santiago* visited the mouth of the Quinault River on the Olympic Peninsula. Negative impressions of the Spanish apparently preceded the arrival of the ship, for the natives attacked and killed members of the crew sent ashore for fresh water.

Initially English sea captains were less active in the Northwest than the Spanish, although as early as 1571 Sir Francis Drake

had sailed along the coast of California and claimed the "Northwest" for England. But the first Europeans actually to occupy the territory were emissaries from Czarist Russia. They had established control over Alaska by the mid eighteenth century and

English Captain James Cook sailed to the Northwest coast in 1776.
Photograph courtesy of the Northwest Collection, Spokane Public Library. Portrait from the Public Archives of Canada.

Captain Robert Gray's ship
Columbia.
Photograph courtesy of the Northwest Collection, Spokane Public Library. From a drawing made in 1792 by George Davidson.

Captain Robert Gray.
Photograph courtesy of the Northwest Collection, Spokane Public Library.

Meriwether Lewis and William Clark.
Photograph courtesy of the Northwest Collection, Spokane Public Library.

or inland waters. Among the latter the Chinook Indians of the Columbia River area controlled a significant portion of white/Indian trade. A center for their trading activity was The Dalles, Oregon, where inland tribes from Canada to California and east to the Great Plains converged in late summer and early fall. The Chinook developed a commercial language that was a blend of words from Spanish, English, Russian, and their own native tongue. The Yakimas participated in these gatherings, and obtained access through the Chinooks to guns, knives, and other goods of European and American manufacture.

operated a series of trading posts all along the Pacific coast. During the last quarter of the eighteenth century, a heightened interest in both exploration and trade brought greater numbers of Spanish, Russian, and English vessels to the Northwest. Serious exploration by the English awaited Captain James Cook, who reached Nootka Sound in 1778. By this time, knowledge of the coast had grown considerably, and captains came more for trade than for exploration.

After American independence, it was only a few years until U.S. ships began to outnumber British vessels in Northwest waters. The Spanish, although first in the region, soon were eclipsed by their Anglo-Saxon counterparts. Among these was the Bostonian Captain Robert Gray, who in 1792 became the first known white man to discover and successfully navigate the Columbia River. It is doubtful that the change of nationalities made much difference to the Indians who engaged in trade, for their experience with whites of whatever origin taught them to be cautious.

Most Indian dealings with whites at the close of the eighteenth century were conducted by those tribes with access to coastal

A Century of Decimation and Defeat

For the inland tribes, the long period of isolation from whites came to an end just after 1800. The American explorers Lewis and Clark descended the Snake and Columbia rivers in 1805, and they were soon followed by American, French Canadian, and British trappers and traders. As a rule, the trappers were treated cordially by natives who shared with them an ambulatory and largely outdoor style of life. So too were Jesuit missionaries who approached the natives with respect and sought to integrate Catholic Christianity with patterns of native religious belief.

Clark

Lewis

This is an artist's rendition of Waiilatpu or Whitman Mission, prior to 1847.
Photograph courtesy of the Northwest Collection, Spokane Public Library.

But even under the most peaceful circumstances, native contact with whites condemned many Indians to death. The chief culprit was white men's diseases to which Indians had no natural resistance. These began to take a toll on the population of the Yakimas and other tribes as early as 1775. But the decimation accelerated in the 1830s and 1840s after Protestant missionaries like Marcus Whitman encouraged white immigration. As a result of his efforts, hundreds of white settlers followed the Oregon Trail each year to the Pacific Northwest. Whitman's mission near Walla Walla became a welcome resting place for weary travelers en route to the Willamette Valley.

This development alone was alarming to Northwest Indians. It fueled distrust of Protestant missionaries, who, in comparison to the paternalism of the "black robes" or Jesuits, were often more confrontational in their attitudes toward native religious and cultural values. But the final straw was an outbreak of measles that white settlers brought to the Whitman mission in 1847. After many Indian children died from the disease, some members of the local Cayuse band, perhaps thinking their children poisoned, attacked the mission and killed its inhabitants. The incident was one element of a circle of violence that did not end until white Americans completed their subjugation of the native populations.

In hindsight it is apparent that the final destiny of the Oregon country was decided early in the national history of the United States. Thomas Jefferson's purchase in 1803 of French claims to "Louisiana"—a vast territory that included the entire Mississippi and Missouri river drainages—set the stage for United States domination of the North American continent from shore to shore. In this precedent-setting acquisition, the region's native peoples were neither consulted nor compensated. Only later, as white Americans sought to occupy the choicest land, would representatives of the United States offer some recognition to Indian rights. The treaties that resulted reflected an ideology of cultural and racial superiority that national leaders used to justify relentless westward expansion.

The first to suffer from this policy were Indian peoples in the Atlantic states, the South, and the Midwest; they were followed by Mexicans in Texas and California in the 1840s. By this time the phrase "manifest destiny" had entered the collective vocabulary. This was an ideology that held that the United States had a predetermined cosmic or spiritual mission to create a continental empire in North America.

The years leading up to the Mexican-American War of 1846–48 provided just the occasion for giving expression to the sentiment that motivated the political and commercial leadership of the United States. Historian Howard Zinn has offered the following samples of the rhetoric that served to rally popular support for that conflict in his *People's History of the United States*:

"Speaking of California, the *Illinois State Register* asked: 'Shall this garden of beauty be suffered to lie dormant in its wild and useless luxuriance? . . . myriads of enterprising Americans would flock to its rich and inviting prairies; the hum of Anglo-Saxon industry would be heard in its valleys; cities would rise upon its plains and seacoast, and the resources and wealth of the nation be increased in an incalculable degree.' The *American Review* talked of Mexicans yielding to 'a superior population, insensibly oozing into her territories, changing her customs, and out-living, out-trading, ex-

terminating her weaker blood. . . .' The New York *Herald* was saying, by 1847: 'The universal Yankee nation can regenerate and disenthrall the people of Mexico in a few years; and we believe it is a part of our destiny to civilize that beautiful country.'

"A letter appeared in the *New York Journal of Commerce* introducing God into the situation: 'The supreme Ruler of the universe seems to interpose, and aid the energy of man towards benefiting mankind. His interposition . . . seems to me to be identified with the success of our arms. . . . That the redemption of 7,000,000 of souls from all the vices that infest the human race, is the ostensible object . . . appears manifest.'"[2]

Although national attention during the early 1840s was directed more toward Texas, California, and Mexico, the Oregon boundary question provided a political platform to presidential candidate James K. Polk in 1844. In that year he urged Americans to perfect their claim to all the Pacific Northwest south of Alaska.

The unresolved border was a result of con-

Jesuit Pierre Jean De Smet posed with numerous Indian chiefs at a peace conference with General Harney at Vancouver in 1858.

Photograph courtesy of the Northwest Collection, Spokane Public Library.

flicting United States and British claims to the region. Oregon was not included in Jefferson's famed Louisiana purchase because that territory stopped at the crest of the Rocky Mountains. But the United States had a claim, based in part upon the discovery of the Columbia River by American Robert Gray, by the explorations in 1805–06 of Lewis and Clark, and by the foundation by American traders of Astoria in 1811. The political problem that remained was the northern limit of Oregon and the validity of British claims to all land north of the Columbia River.

In the early decades of the nineteenth century, the disputed territory attracted few permanent white settlers. Indians were the principal occupants of the land that became Washington state, along with French and English speaking traders from British North America whose primary commercial centers were situated at Vancouver, Nisqually, and in the eastern portion of the territory, at Colville and Spokane.

By 1844, when Polk ran for president, an influential segment of public opinion supported the extension of vast territorial claims for the United States and the exclusion from

This is a Hollywood replication of a typical wagon train—like the many that followed the Oregon Trail to the Northwest.
Photograph courtesy of the Museum of History & Industry.

North America of citizens of other nations. Polk appealed to this opinion in 1844 through his campaign promise to extend U.S. claims in Oregon territory to "Fifty-four forty or fight." This catchy phrase signified depriving the British of the entire northwest coast of North America up to the southern limit—established by treaty with the Czar in 1824—of Russian Alaska.

Had President Polk not been otherwise occupied in his war against Mexico, his election campaign rhetoric might have led to a serious confrontation with the British in the Northwest. By treaty with Britain in 1819, the United States' claim to "Oregon" was recognized. No boundaries with English settlements in the Northwest were immediately fixed, and U.S. leaders rejected a British proposal in 1825 to extend the boundary along the forty-ninth parallel from the crest of the Rocky Mountains to its point of intersection with the Columbia River, and thence following that course to the sea. But in 1846 President Polk accepted a modification of this suggestion by which the United States gained undivided control over all territories south of the forty-ninth parallel that lay east of the Strait of Georgia's main channel.

U.S. Army General Isaac Stevens (seated) is photographed with his staff circa 1860.
Photograph courtesy of the Northwest Collection, Spokane Public Library. From *The Life of Isaac Stevens*, by his son Hazard Stevens.

The decade of the 1840s was already significant in terms of the numbers of Americans emigrating to Oregon. But after 1846 many more Americans felt free to settle north of the Columbia River, in a territory heretofore largely administered as a private holding of the British-American Hudson Bay Company. South of the Columbia River, the population grew sufficiently by 1848 to warrant the designation of Oregon as a U.S. territory, with a capital at Oregon City. The new territorial government had jurisdiction over the entire northwest region until 1853 when Oregon Territory was reduced to the size of the present state and Washington Territory was established.

Washington Territory's first governor was Isaac Stevens, a young, ambitious military man from Andover, Massachusetts. His initial responsibilities included overseeing the establishment of U.S. territorial government, making treaties with the Indian tribes and freeing land for white settlement, and surveying optimal routes for a northern continental railway. The enormous potential for conflict of interest in these separate roles was not politically significant during the nineteenth century and went unchallenged, if not unnoticed.

The major agenda item for Stevens in his new job was dealing with the Indians. The general approach that Stevens took in the task had been determined by patterns already established at mid century by the United States in its treaties with Indian nations in other parts of the country. The government's primary objective was to obtain a legal transfer of land from the Indians to the federal government, and in return to establish Indian reservations, to provide compensation for land ceded, and to guarantee rights for the pursuit of traditional Indian livelihoods.

Stevens pursued his treaty-making mission with zeal, and by 1855 had acquired signatures from many of the region's chiefs or from Indians claiming to have the power to act as chiefs. For central and southern Washington, the principal gathering occurred in June at Walla Walla. Three major treaties resulted. Stevens' treaty with the Yakimas included, in addition to Yakimas under Kamiakin, delegates from the Palouse, Pisquouse, Wenatshapam, Klickitat, Klinquit, Kow-was-say-ee, Li-ay-was, Skin-pah, Wish-ham, Shyiks, Ochechotes, Kah-milt-pah, and Se-ap-cat. Their territory, which was conveyed by the treaty to the United States of America, included all of the land east of the Cascade summit from the Columbia River on the south to the Methow River on the north (i.e., excluding most of Okanogan county), as far east as 119 degrees, 10 minutes west longitude (approximately the boundary between Grant and Lincoln counties), and excluding on the south the land now included in Benton county.

In return for this cession, the treaty provided the confederated tribes and bands (for convenience referred to collectively as Yakimas) with a reservation bounded on the west by the crest of the Cascade Mountains and on the east by the Yakima River between the Ahtanum River and a ridge intersecting the Yakima River eight miles south of Satus Creek. The reservation was for the sole use and occupation of the Indians, and white men were specifically excluded without permission of the tribe and Indian superintendent.

The treaty detailed other compensation as well. Payment to Indians was made for improvements which they abandoned off reservation lands, and for relocating to the reservation. Other funds were to be provided for "breaking up and fencing farms, building houses for them, supplying them with provisions and a suitable outfit, and for such other objects as [the President of the United States] shall deem necessary." Other sums were designated for annuities to be paid during a twenty-year period beginning in 1856.

The treaty also promised construction of two schools, one for agriculture and one for industry, and various shops for blacksmiths, gunsmiths, wheelwrights, and carpenters, all fully equipped and staffed; and the construction of a sawmill, flourmill, and a hospital equipped with medicine and staffed with a physician. Other provisions pledged surveying services for Indians wishing to make "permanent" homes, stipulated the prohibition of alcohol, and allocated a one-township tract for a fishery on the Columbia at the mouth of the Wenatshapam [Wenatchee] River.

A further provision, and one that would cause great controversy more than a century later, read as follows:

"The exclusive right of taking fish in all the streams, where running through or bordering said reservation, is further secured to said confederated tribes and bands of Indians, as also the right of taking fish at all usual and accustomed places, in common with the citizens of the Territory, and of erecting temporary buildings for curing them; together with the privilege of hunting, gathering roots and berries, and pasturing their horses and cattle upon open and unclaimed land."[3]

Some white Americans perhaps believed these treaties to represent fair exchanges. However, most individuals who were close to the negotiations recognized that the value to white settlers of Indian lands far exceeded the amount of monetary compensation offered the tribes. Several decades later, a white pioneer calculated the cost to the government for the Walla Walla treaties at approximately $650,000, mostly in annuities. "Thus for a mere pittance, in comparison with its present value, was secured from the

Native Americans fish at the Columbia River's Celilo Falls.
Photograph courtesy of the Yakima Nation Library.

Indians this possessory right to a large portion of eastern Oregon and Washington and northern Idaho, a region rich in wealth already acquired and still richer in its possibilities."[4] The loss to native Americans was more than financial. Many understood the treaties, which masqueraded as equitable barter, to be an impermissible and sacrilegious alienation of a birthright.

Neither side fully realized what the future course of events would bring. Policy makers in Washington, D.C., were motivated by well-meaning though totally misplaced altruism, as well as by chauvinism, racism, and greed. These elements assumed different proportions in different persons, depending upon individual characters, but coexisted in most. The result was attempts to implement an Indian policy that had at its core the idea that native Americans could be remade as farmers and workers in the white mold—in a word, "civilized."

Part of the problem was weakness on the part of Bureau of Indian Affairs personnel, who, for example, had to be admonished as early as 1861 not to keep Indian concubines. But the larger problem was the misguided nature of the policy itself, which failed to recognize fundamental cultural, religious, and intellectual values that together shaped native American character. In its futile attempt to assimilate Indians to white ways, children were compelled to attend military-type boarding schools, the nation's first example of which was created in 1860 on the Yakima reservation. There children were isolated from their families, forced to speak only English, and denied freedom to prac-

Native American school children stand in a group at Fort Simcoe on the Yakima reservation, circa 1900.

Photograph courtesy of the Yakima Nation Library. From the Harvey Wolfe Collection.

Yakima chief George Maninich (center) confers with other members of the tribe and an attorney (at his left).

Photograph courtesy of the Northwest Collection, Spokane Public Library. Teakle Collection.

Native American children stand outside a log school building.
Photograph courtesy of the Northwest Collection, Spokane Public Library.

tice their aboriginal religions. The policy was an attempt at social engineering that was doomed from the start to failure.

Native American Responses

Given the extent and rapidity with which white Americans established political and military control over the land that became the state of Washington, it is understandable that native Americans should rise in protest. The first manifestations of displeasure at the terms of white settlement were registered during treaty negotiations in 1855 with Governor Stevens. At Walla Walla, Chief Kamiakin of the Yakimas reportedly bit his lip so hard that it bled as he signed the treaty, and at Medicine Creek, in western Washington, Chief Leschi was said to have ripped up the treaty document and stormed off. On the other hand, some tribal representatives were attracted by the promises of the white man's technology and enticed by the what seemed to be large sums of money, and signed willingly. But others saw further than the temptation of immediate gain. Chief Looking Glass of the Nez Perce, who arrived late to the negotiations at Walla Walla, was recorded as saying "My people, what have you done? While I was gone you sold my country."[5]

Even though native Americans outnumbered white settlers in Washington by an approximate ratio of four to one in 1855, there is clear evidence that the Indian population had been declining since contact with whites, mainly due to deaths from disease. Many Indian leaders recognized this, and some were fatalistic about their people's prospects for the future. This probably explains in part why so few combatants—no more than several hundred out of a statewide population of approximately twelve thousand native Americans—participated in the "Indian Wars" of 1855 to 1858.

The "Indian Wars" of the 1850s were more properly speaking a series of isolated battles that started in the fall of 1855 to protest the conditions of Governor Stevens' treaties.

Although some of the early skirmishes occurred in western Washington, the principal battlegrounds were in eastern Washington. Here Indian forces, generally led by the Yakima Chief Kamiakin, inflicted more than one defeat upon the United States Army. Although outnumbered by Indians, the whites had superior firepower, disease, technology, and a rising tide of population in their favor. The final battle, waged in 1858 near Spokane, only sealed a fate that to many seemed predetermined. At this engagement the Indian forces were first pinned to an inferior position, then encircled, and finally captured. Twelve Indian war leaders were executed, though Kamiakin himself escaped.

The desultory resistance that Chief Kamiakin and others offered during the mid 1850s ended any real military opposition to

A Washington coastal Indian woman in 1910 carries a load of sticks.
Photograph courtesy of the Northwest Collection, Spokane Public Library. Photograph by Asahel Curtis.

white occupation of Washington Territory. Most later battles were isolated incidents that served mainly to reinforce among whites stereotyped images of native savagery than to advance any specific military cause of the Indians. The heroic stands during the 1870s of Chief Joseph of the Nez Perce, for example, are more monuments to his pride and integrity than a calculated element of military strategy.

The effect of the political and military initiatives of the United States government was to subdue the native populations of Washington. In central Washington, this meant relocating Indians to the Yakima and Colville reservations, and beginning a program of economic and cultural "reeducation."

For many reasons, the initial attempts of the Bureau of Indian Affairs to promote the assimilation of native Americans into white society did not produce their intended results. This failure gave political ammunition to proponents of change in federal policy towards Indians, even when these changes held the potential for further degradation of economic, social, and physical and mental health conditions among native American groups.

From the economic point of view, the most important change in Indian policy was the enactment by Congress of the Dawes Act of 1887. This legislation replaced collective ownership of reservation lands with allotments to individual tribal members. The result was a massive transfer of the best Indian lands to white settlers, and a further impoverishment of Indian tribes. By the time Congress repealed this act in 1934, as much as two-thirds of the nation's reservation lands had been acquired by non-Indians. In the case of the Yakima reservation, this included much of the valley's most productive orchard lands.

In north central Washington, the United States established a Colville Indian Reservation in the northeastern corner of the state in 1872. But the immediate protests of white homesteaders induced the government to move the reservation west to its present location between the Columbia and Okanogan rivers. Twenty years later miners discovered gold in the northern half of the Indian reservation, and Congress bowed to local white interests by taking it back from the Indians and opening it to farming and mining. Eight years later, in 1900, the government declared the southern half of the Colville reservation open to white settlement as well. As a result, non-Indians now own half the lands in the reservation.

During the twentieth century U.S. policy towards Indians and tribes changed directions on several occasions. In 1924 Congress granted American citizenship to Indians, while specifying explicitly that the new status did not diminish in any way Indian treaty rights. During the mid 1930s Congress repealed the Dawes Act, and the Roosevelt administration encouraged the revitalization of tribal government. Twenty years later the government abruptly reversed course by proposing to terminate tribal governments and abolish reservations. The plan was scotched only after Indian leaders protested vigorously.

The history of federal policy toward the Indians since the treaties of the mid ninteenth century is important for understanding the legal issues of the 1970s and 1980s regarding the allocation of fish and water in the areas drained by the Columbia River and its tributaries. It is also vital for assessing the political agendas of Indian tribes in the contemporary period.

Three Yakima women witness the inundation of Celilo Falls on 10 March 1957.
Photograph courtesy of the Yakima Nation Library.

CHAPTER 3

The Pioneer Era

The conclusion of the Indian Wars in 1858 was followed a year later by Congressional ratification of the treaties of 1855 and a presidential proclamation that officially opened lands in eastern Oregon and Washington to settlement. These actions encouraged some men living in Oregon's Willamette Valley to settle near Walla Walla in southeastern Washington or around Goldendale in the Klickitat Valley. Here they found land in plenty for cattle raising and a measure of solitude that was attractive to many individuals living on the frontier.

It was only a matter of time until early pioneers would judge even the sparsely settled Klickitat Valley to be "overcrowded," and extend the frontier further. Such an individual was Fielding M. Thorp, who moved his family and cattle to the Yakima Valley in 1861. In time Thorp's settlement became Moxee City, a small community located a few miles west of the Yakima River near the mouth of Ahtanum Creek. Two years later the territorial legislature decided to endow the area with local government.

"Ferguson County" was the result, but the few white residents living in the area were not impressed. According to A. J. Splawn, who came to the area as a young man, "the settlers did not need it. They had protected themselves up to this time and felt they were abundantly able so to do for a number of years to come. What money they got from time to time they very much needed for their own support, and did not feel like being taxed for the upkeep of a bunch of office holders over at Olympia."[1]

In 1865 the legislature reduced the size of the county somewhat, but the residents continued to place few demands on county officials and whatever taxation existed was mostly voluntary. Self-help and neighborly assistance remained not only the underlying ethic but the only practical means for getting along. The year 1875 provided an example of how residents could convert this spirit into action. Yakima Valley settlers built a wagon road that year to the summit of the Simcoe Mountains to connect with a similar project undertaken by residents of the Klickitat Valley on the other side. As a result, communication with Goldendale and and the Columbia River improved considerably.

Already by 1870, however, Fielding Thorp had concluded that the Yakima Valley had too many people to suit him. He packed up, and following the trail taken in 1869 by approximately two dozen other pioneer settlers, established his final residence on Taneum Creek in the Kittitas Valley. Until about 1860 the region was unoccupied by whites. Then a small trading post at the ford near the mouth of Manashtash Creek began serving Indians and a very limited number of whites who ventured across the territory. The first permanent settlers, however, were described by Splawn as "two wanderers, Frederick Ludi and John Galler," who located just south of the present city of

Ellensburg in 1867.

According to Splawn, everyone in the Kittitas Valley "was in the cattle business" during the seventies, partly because almost no market existed for agricultural products. Supplies for the store that Splawn opened in Ellensburg in 1870 still came mainly from The Dalles, since no wagon road existed across Snoqualmie Pass. This was the Kittitas Valley's prime era for cowboys, a period when stockmen drove both cattle and sheep across the mountains to Puget Sound markets and as far east as Montana and Wyoming. But the economic predominance of cattle ended with the hard winter of 1880–81, when cold and starvation decimated herds across eastern Oregon and Washington. Some stockmen did not recover from their losses, and the valley during the early eighties began to attract farmers and miners as well as ranchers.

One newcomer to the upper Kittitas Valley who preserved and then enhanced the area's reputation for livestock raising was James Masterson, a relative of Dodge City, Kansas's famous marshal, Bat Masterson.

According to oral tradition, James Masterson acquired his land near the settlement of Teanaway in 1880 from an Indian named Chief Pohasti for six deerskins and a plug of tobacco.[2] In the ensuing years Masterson laid the foundations for the family's prominence in cattle raising and breeding. He also profited from the construction of the Northern Pacific Railway, by obtaining a contract to supply ties from Cle Elum to Easton and beyond.

Settling the Upper Valley

Within a very short period of time, a community had grown into existence in the immediate vicinity of the Masterson ranch. This was Teanaway, located near the confluence of the Teanaway and Yakima rivers. The site was a natural point of departure for persons headed for any of three areas: the upper Yakima Valley to the west and the smaller Teanaway Valley and Swauk Prairie areas to the north. Until Masterson arrived, the area's principal inhabitants were Yakima Indians of the Kittitas band who by government oversight or insouciance had escaped

Roslyn's oldest structure is a log cabin built around 1880.
Photo by the author.

Farmers harvest wheat in Kittitas Valley, after the turn of the century.
Photograph courtesy of the Museum of History & Industry.

mandatory resettlement to the reservation.

But others had come as well. One was S. S. Hawkins, a prospector who discovered gold and silver in the Cle Elum River in 1880. News of this find encouraged other prospectors to comb the nearby mountains for mineral, and soon the region's lodes of copper were also revealed. But only a handful of pioneers called the upper valley home in the early 1880s. One of the earliest of these was Nez "Cayuse" Jensen, a prospector-homesteader whose log cabin still stands in Roslyn at the corner of Second and Utah. The cabin, which Jensen and friends erected around 1880, is one of the oldest continuously occupied structures in the state. Other early pioneer residents established farms and ranches in a broad arc from Lake Cle Elum all the way to Swauk Prairie, where in September 1883 George Virden

was said to have a "picturesque farm." His neighbors that year with well-improved properties included "Mssrs. Giles, Seaton Senior, and Masterson," as well as a number of "last comers" whose homesteads by comparison were rudimentary.[3]

The valley definitely began to "settle up" during 1883, the year that Thomas Gamble and Walter Reed staked their claims to land five miles west of Teanaway. A correspondent from Teanaway wrote on 1 September 1883 of the bright future of that settlement:

"Several thousand acres of agricultural lands have been located in this region during the present season and thousands of acres of mixed timber and open lands yet remain for settlement. A large mill race has been taken out of the Teanaway and two sawmills and a grist mill are now under construction. The principal settlement lies along and one to four miles away from the Seattle and Walla Walla wagon road, as also of the proposed Cascade division of the Northern Pacific railroad, the 100-mile tree from salt water being located at a point just opposite the mouth of Teanaway creek. At no distant day this must be a large and prosperous settlement, and will add not a little to the traffic of both wagon road and railroad. The heavy snowfall, averaging perhaps three and a half feet, and the supposed prevalence of destructive frosts, have done much to retard the settlement of the Teanaway country, but hardy Minnesotans are filling up the region and are well satisfied."[4]

The optimism of the Teanaway citizen

who penned those lines was misplaced, for he had not reckoned with the ingenuity of Walter Reed. Three years later, as the Northern Pacific began to approach from Ellensburg, Reed combined forces with sawmill owner Thomas Johnson to attract the railroad depot to Cle Elum. By platting the townsite of Cle Elum, and then offering one-half shares of the proceeds from land sales to the Northern Pacific's locating engineers, Reed ensured that future urban settlement would occur on and around his property. Left without a depot, Teanaway soon melted away, to the general benefit of Cle Elum.

For the remainder of the 1880s Cle Elum thrived as the temporary headquarters for the Northern Pacific Railway's Stampede Pass tunnel project. Johnson's sawmill

A drawing depicts Thomas Johnson's Cle Elum sawmill, shortly after 1886.

Photograph courtesy of the Special Collections Division, University of Washington Libraries.

This artist's rendition of the Reed House in Cle Elum was executed during the late 1880s.
Photograph courtesy of the Special Collections Division, University of Washington Libraries.

This picture of the 1908 flood shows an early Northern Pacific depot at "Clealum."
Photograph courtesy of Albert Schober.

hummed with activity providing lumber for construction, while the Reed House maintained a brisk business. Other merchants and innkeepers added to Cle Elum's commercial core, and by 1890 the town had a permanent population of 337 persons. In that year the community erected its first dedicated school building, having outgrown the cabin that Walter Reed initially provided.

Indians within White Communities

At the time that white Americans began to settle the upper valley, Yakima Indians of the Kittitas band had inhabited the area for many centuries. Some of these natives continued to make their homes there even after the government mandated their removal to the newly created reservation in the Yakima

Valley. We do not know the number of Indian family units permanently residing in what became Kittitas County during 1884, but anecdotal evidence suggests that their number was small.

Our sources for information about native Americans in the Cle Elum area following white settlement are limited. They include a warm and personal account of a long life on the frontier written by A. J. Splawn. Splawn was raised in Oregon and moved first to the Klickitat Valley, then to Yakima, and finally to Ellensburg. His career as a Washington pioneer spanned the entire second half of the nineteenth century. Other evidence comes from newspaper accounts and legal records from the 1890s, and from the recollections of long-time resident Bat Masterson, recorded in 1978 by John Deonigi. Still more information from local families is preserved in *Spawn of Coal Dust*.[5]

From the perspective of a mature age, Splawn wrote a sympathetic biography of Chief Kamiakin of the Yakimas and many other Washington Indians. The book presents Kamiakin as the proud representative of an honorable people who valued highly their relationship with kinsmen, nature, and the spirits. In Splawn's account, Kamiakin's heroic resistance to the Walla Walla treaty of 1855 was principled and justifiable, even if in the end it was also futile and personally destructive. By the time Splawn committed his thoughts to writing in the early years of the twentieth century, time and events had reduced the Indian population of Washington to a minority subclass and altered forever the balance of power between the races. His book preserves the perspective of an enlightened pioneer of the mid nineteenth century.

As the nineteenth century advanced and

A recent photograph shows a venerable Yakima sport—horseracing.
Photograph courtesy of the Yakima Nation Library.

*Yakima children play
near the boundary of the
Yakima reservation.*
Photograph courtesy of the
Special Collections Division,
University of Washington
Libraries.

more white Americans moved onto lands once occupied exclusively by Indians, differences in cultural values became more apparent. For example, settlers in the Kittitas Valley brought with them Anglo-Saxon concepts of property rights that had little meaning for Indians. Individual Yakimas did not "own" sections of land as pioneer Americans wanted to do, rather they lived on the land and shared collectively in what must have seemed to be an inexhaustible natural bounty. Thus, when James Masterson "purchased" his ranch from Chief Pohasti for six deerskins and a plug of tobacco, the recipient of these items probably viewed them as payment for nonexclusive use of the land, for how could he alienate something he did not individually own? Nonetheless, fences soon went up and as the century wore to a close, Indians living in white society increasingly had to adjust to the newcomer's ways.

Some evidence for this adjustment comes from the Masterson ranch, where Indians—like John Quititit and his family—were sometimes hired to perform chores. This "Indian John," the person for whom the hill east of Cle Elum and the Interstate-90 rest area was named, had taken out a homestead on a quarter section of land that spanned both sides of the Yakima River at the base of the hill. In a limited way the family participated in the community economy, John by growing vegetables to sell in Cle Elum, his wife by doing washing for the Sasse Hotel.

Other Indians also participated in the money economy of the whites by taking occasional odd jobs. But for the most part they continued to live from traditional hunting,

fishing, and gathering activities. As a result, they were visible to whites in the budding towns of Roslyn and Cle Elum in the late 1880s and during the 1890s, but remained outsiders who were often feared or shunned. These are the underlying attitudes that caused young children who encountered John Quititit's wife in Cle Elum to tease and throw rocks at her, or that caused the widow of Roslyn miner Thomas Brennan, a transplanted Missourian, to fear that passing Indians had "child stealing" in mind.

Occasionally the Indians who lived in the upper valley around the turn of the century found friends among white residents. One such individual was Henry Kitchen, who lived in Roslyn from 1886 until his death in the mines in 1893. According to family tradition, recorded in *Spawn of Coal Dust*, Kitchen was "a good friend of the Indians who lived around here at the time. They were saddened by his death." Anita Baker Fera recalled that her father, Thornton Baker, came to central Washington in 1880 from the East and spent several years as a cowboy before settling in Roslyn. "He knew the Columbia Basin like a book" and could read Indian petroglyphs. He had "many friends among the Indians and he had shared many a camp site with them." Her childhood memories included the sight of Indians stopping to talk with her father. She recalled that they spoke in "strange sounds that didn't mean a thing to us."[6]

Year by year the native American presence in the upper valley dwindled, until the last members of the Kittitas band died around 1910. The world had changed greatly for native Americans during the nineteenth century. That was an era when "every American cliche ran in reverse: expansion became contraction, democracy became tyranny, prosperity became poverty, and liberty became confinement."[7] In one sense, however, relegation to the reservation provided some benefits to the Yakima Indian Nation. A people has survived, and is likely to survive for years to come.

Hostility Toward the Chinese

The Chinese who came to work in the United States during the second half of the nineteenth century encountered strong racial prejudice. They had come in large numbers to build the nation's railroads, particularly in the West. But white workers in America resented the fact that they were willing to labor at starvation wages under almost intolerable conditions, and lobbied successfully for a federal law that excluded

Chinese from citizenship and barred any new Chinese immigration after 1882.

In Washington state anti-Chinese sentiment grew during the mid 1880s. Chinese communities and groups of workers faced discrimination, demonstrations, and sometimes riots and other acts of violence. In Kittitas County, prospectors who

Indian petroglyphs are found frequently on hills above the Columbia River.
Photograph courtesy of the Northwest Collection, Spokane Public Library. From the Teakle Collection.

organized mining laws for the Swauk district in 1884 stipulated that "Chinamen were forbidden to come into, mine, or hold property in the camp."[8] In Seattle, whites took direct action in 1886 to remove Chinese residents from their homes and to force them on a steamer bound for San Francisco. When local and state authorities intervened, a riot broke out that left one white demonstrator dead and three others wounded.

Meanwhile Chinese work gangs helped to secure the early opening of the Northern Pacific Railway's Cascade branch. After this work was completed in 1887, white prospectors recruited a group of twenty-five Chinese to work placer mines located north of the Salmon la Sac guard station. The Chinese lived at a place called China Camp, until they fell victim to a massacre that left all but one dead. The murderers escaped justice, and in the course of time a folk legend arose that attributed responsibility for the massacre to Yakima Indians.[9]

It is far more likely, however, that whites were responsible. Some evidence for this hypothesis is found in *Spawn of Coal Dust*, where it was said of early Roslyn resident William Rees that "he can tell some real stories about how they drove the Chinamen out of the mines."[10]

It was common practice among the Chinese in the United States to live and work in groups. But some adventurous individuals broke this pattern by establishing laundries or Chinese restaurants. The China Camp survivor, "Challie Sam"—as he was known to many Roslyn whites—was reportedly a founder of the New York Cafe in Ellensburg. Other Chinese operated a laundry in Cle Elum until after the turn of the century. However, the 1900 census did not reveal any Chinese inhabitants in Roslyn, a situation perhaps linked to the well-known anti-Chinese sentiment of such early labor unions as the Knights of Labor.

The drawing on the opposite page documents the anti-Chinese riot in Seattle in 1886.
Photograph courtesy of the Museum of History & Industry. Drawing by W. P. Snyder.

CHAPTER 4

Railroad!

After a long period of isolation from the advancing United States, that part of the west that bordered the Cascade Mountains on the west, the Rockies on the east, and the Blue Mountains on the south, was secure in the hands of pioneer American citizens. The land provided a sufficient though simple living for its new owners, as virgin meadows yielded to the plow and forests gave up their trees for cabins, fence posts, and firewood. But the region promised far more than subsistence farming. With a steadily rising population to create markets, and a rapidly developing transportation system to transfer resources economically, many more thousands of individuals could share in the Northwest's natural bounty.

The railroad magnates of the 1870s and 1880s grasped this potential far better than most. Unsurpassed as publicists for the region, their agents combed northern and central Europe for immigrants, sparing no arguments to persuade individuals and even entire communities to relocate to the great Northwest. Their work fulfilled many objectives. It served the national policy of the United States, which sought to expand across the continent. It furthered "progress," as measured in terms of national agricultural and industrial outputs. It also created impressive fortunes for individuals like Henry Villard and James J. Hill who possessed both the vision and the acumen to organize, promote, and build integrated

transportation and natural resource empires that stretched from the Great Lakes to the Pacific Northwest.

Laying iron rails across the prairies was a bold undertaking that carried huge risks for both financiers and their legions of bond-holders. The fortunes of Philadelphian banker Jay Cooke had crumbled in 1873 as a result of the bankruptcy of the Northern Pacific Railroad. Cooke owed this disaster in part to corruption and mismanagement, but also to America's impatience for progress and unrealistic expectations for transcontinental railway systems. During this period when western railroads traversed vast wildernesses that generated little or no traffic, financial viability depended in large measure upon the willingness of creditors to trade present returns for future value. The panic of 1873 can be explained in part by the excessive investment of cash resources in capital projects like railroads, whose operating profits were too low even to service their debt.

The collapse of Jay Cooke and the financial panic that resulted in 1873 allowed a German emigre by the name of Henry Villard to acquire the Northern Pacific with borrowed money for just cents on the dollar. He was keenly aware of the need to bring settlers to the Pacific Northwest. As related by one historian, Villard

". . . filled the entire world with his pictures, stereopticon slides and 'literature' illustrating the Eden-like

This drawing shows the Northern Pacific's first mine at Roslyn, soon after 1886 (on facing page).
Photograph courtesy of the Special Collections Division, University of Washington Libraries.

northwestern territories. Hundreds of his immigration agents spread their dragnet throughout Europe and England, hauling the peasants from Germany and Sweden in by the thousands to Oregon and the Columbia Basin; depopulating sometimes whole villages in Russia."[1]

People flocked to the Northwest in unprecedented numbers during the decade that saw the completion of the first northern tier railroad. In the space of ten years, from 1880 to 1890, the number of residents in Washington grew nearly fivefold from 75,116 to 357,232. New towns sprouted all along the rail lines, and for the first time more than a third of the state's inhabitants made their livings in urban environments. The founding of Roslyn and Cle Elum in 1886 took place during this substantial tide of migration into Washington Territory, partly as a direct result of choices made by executive officers of the Northern Pacific Railway.

Long before the last spike joined the Northern Pacific's western and eastern lines in 1883, the holders of the railroad's charter had envisaged building across the Cascades to Puget Sound. This project was deferred

until last because existing steamship routes through the Columbia River Gorge made it possible for passengers and freight to reach Portland from the head of navigation near Pasco. A branch line from Vancouver to Tacoma completed the transcontinental connection for Puget Sound communities. Ultimately, the question was not whether the Cascade line would be constructed, but where. Survey reports going back to 1869 suggested routes from as far south as Cowlitz Pass to as far north as Stevens Pass. However, the final selection of a route was not made until after 1880.

In the fall of 1880 V. G. Bogue, a Northern Pacific locating engineer, departed Portland with a survey team to begin an examination of Cascade passes. The Stampede Pass route, which Bogue discovered in March 1881, became his first choice for the railway right-of-way. In August of 1882 Bogue returned with assistant engineer J. L. Kingsbury to locate a tunnel near the summit of the pass. This route won the approval of the Northern Pacific's board of directors later that year.

But during the short-lived presidency of Henry Villard, from 1881 to January, 1884, the project of constructing a rail route across

V. G. Bogue's survey party assembled in 1880, and later discovered Stampede Pass.

Photograph courtesy of the Washington State Historical Society.

*Northern Pacific con-
struction engineers and
crews camp near the
summit of Stampede Pass
in 1886.*
Photograph courtesy of the
Yakima Valley Museum &
Historical Association. (Gibson
album).

*A Northern Pacific
Railway pile driver
builds progressively
across the Naches River.*
Photograph courtesy of the
Yakima Valley Museum &
Historical Association. (Gibson
album).

the Cascades occupied a third-place priority behind completing the transcontinental link between Spokane and eastern Montana and protecting the shipping monopoly of Villard's Oregon Railway & Navigation Company along the Columbia River. There

would be time later for a direct link from Wallula Junction (near Pasco) to Seattle or Tacoma.

Some work was undertaken as early as the summer of 1883 on a portion of the line from Yakima to Ellensburg, although the

This portal shows construction at the eastern end of the Stampede Pass tunnel project.
Photograph courtesy of the Yakima Valley Museum & Historical Association. (Gibson album).

main drive for completion began only in December 1884. By this time Villard had departed, and with him the prospects for a Northern Pacific domination of the Columbia River traffic corridor. The Cascade branch was now assured its place as part of the Northern Pacific main line.[2]

It is part of local legend that boosters of the upper Kittitas valley had a role to play in deciding whether the Northern Pacific would take a Stampede Pass or a Natches Pass route across the Cascades. In this version of events, the railroad's management remained undecided until local residents informed them of the discovery of a high quality seam of coal near Roslyn's future townsite. Although railroad experts did not arrive to look over this field until 1886, word of the discovery nonetheless tipped the scales in favor of a route through Ellensburg and Cle Elum.[3]

The notion that the discovery of coal determined the railroad's route is certainly plausible. But examined in the light of known facts, it appears that Roslyn's wealth of coal contributed little or nothing to the choice of Cascade routes. Instead, the decision appeared to turn more on the matter of the elevation of passes, the straightness and grade of the approaches to the summit, and the number of bridges, trestles, and tunnels that would be required to lay the track. Construction expense was a major consideration, along with directness of route to Puget Sound from the railroad's western terminus at Wallula Junction.

There is some evidence that the Northern Pacific was aware of early reports of coal "float" in the Cle Elum area. One historical account even asserts that around 1881 the railroad sent a prospecting party, headed by a man named Taylor, to investigate the region. But "the party failed to discover the desired commodity, and had the assurance to report the utter absence of it in the country."[4] Given the conclusion of the report, it is unlikely that Taylor's investigation prompted Bogue to recommend the Stampede Pass route. And it is a certainty that the Northern Pacific was not swayed by information obtained from Thomas Gamble, Walter Reed, or C. P. Brosius, for the latter staked their homesites in Cle Elum and Roslyn in the year following the railroad's decision.

These seven men discovered the Roslyn coal field for the Northern Pacific Railway in May 1886.
Photograph courtesy of the Special Collections Division, University of Washington Libraries.

We may never reconstruct how much was known about the Roslyn field's coal resources in the period prior to 1883, and thus fully resolve the question about the Northern Pacific's choice of routes. A geologist working for Washington state around 1912 interviewed pioneers on this subject, and concluded that "no authentic report of the earliest discovery of coal in Kittitas County has been found, although inquiry has been made of many of the oldest settlers."[5] One of his sources, Isaiah Buchanan, claimed to have known about coal in the Roslyn area as early as 1871 or 1872. If so, he apparently was not impressed with its potential, for he chose to take up land on Manashtash Creek instead. Later he worked some prospect mines there and removed some coal, but the workings were not of a high enough quality to merit full commercial exploitation.

Only after the Northern Pacific line was laid as far west as Ellensburg did the North-

ern Pacific send a survey party to Cle Elum to prospect the field. The seven men who arrived in May 1886 were H. E. Graham, Harry Cottle, Thomas Fleming, Archibald Patrick, William Thompson, Archie Anderson, and William Anderson. Their exploration included sinking prospect holes east and west from Cle Elum, from the Masterson ranch to the future site of Roslyn. Although the discovery of the Roslyn vein did not affect the Northern Pacific's choice of routes, it did change the railroad's construction priorities and decided the future of the region.

Beginning in August, a crew of eighteen men worked at breakneck speed to develop the railroad's trove of "black diamonds." Although in a race to complete the Cascade line to the Sound, the Northern Pacific gave immediate attention to constructing the new Roslyn branch line and developing its coal workings. Logan M. Bullitt, vice-president of the Northern Pacific Coal Company,

A Chinese work party shovels snow in the winter of 1886 to enable tracklayers to proceed across Stampede Pass.
Photograph courtesy of the Yakima Valley Museum & Historical Association. (Gibson album).

directed the work. While Chinese laborers laid rails to Roslyn, the carpenters that he sent from St. Paul constructed a sawmill to provide timbers for the mines and lumber for their outside structures.

Cle Elum became the first platted townsite in the area when local residents Walter J. Reed and his wife Barbara A. Reed filed a plat on 26 July with the county auditor. The initial townsite included the land just past Billings Avenue on the west to a line east of Bullitt Avenue between the railroad and just beyond Fourth Street. The Reeds had arrived in Cle Elum from Pennsylvania in 1883, and had settled just west of their friend Thomas Gamble.

Roslyn's foundation followed on 22 September when a town plat was presented to county officials in Ellensburg. The community's borders at first encompassed land from First to Third streets. It was limited by Utah on the north, and on the south by Montana (between First and Second) and Dakota (between Second and Third). Unlike Cle Elum, Roslyn was laid out in an odd-numbered section—hence on land that would become part of the Northern Pacific land grant. The town received its name from Bullitt, who by one account was inspired by the Delaware birthplace of a fair maiden he loved, or by another account wished to honor the place of residence of a New York friend.[6]

The incorporation of Roslyn as a town

under the laws of Washington Territory followed in February 1889, when residents organized to install a community water system. At this time Roslyn was already a bustling mining town, but Cle Elum contained "little more than a sawmill and a few houses" until the mid nineties. By that time Roslyn had already become a focal point for labor unrest that resulted in a legal showdown between the territorial government and officials of the Northern Pacific Railway.

Labor Strife in Roslyn

Mining coal was the company's top priority in 1886, and by 14 December the first loads of coal were dumped over the tipple and sent out of Roslyn to fuel the railroad's motive power. While work still progressed on closing the final link in the main line across Stampede Pass during the spring of 1887, the railroad extended its Roslyn branch line north to the present site of Ronald and began to develop its Number 3 mine, aided

by a new contingent of four hundred Italian miners brought in during the fall of 1886. By the start of 1888, Roslyn was transformed from a temporary mining camp into a community with as many as twelve hundred inhabitants.

At the start Roslyn was a company town owned and managed by the Northern Pacific Coal Company. Its officials clearly wanted Roslyn to become a permanent community, and the home for hard working and peaceful mining families. The objectives were met, but not without some strife that probably was not a part of the company's original plan for Roslyn's development.

The miners who flocked to Roslyn from all parts of the United States also brought with them aspirations for improved working conditions, better pay, and an eight-hour working day. To achieve their objectives, activist miners advocated the establishment of a labor union. By 1888 a Knights of Labor union hall had opened, and in the summer the area's first labor dispute confronted the

The town of Roslyn photographed in 1889 already showed substantial development.
Photograph courtesy of the Roslyn Museum.

This photo shows Albert Loska, a railroad section foreman, inspecting track circa 1905.
Photograph courtesy of Albert Schober.

management of the Northern Pacific. The principal issue was the miners' demand for an eight-hour day.

Because Northern Pacific management refused either to recognize the Knights of Labor or to bargain with the miners, a strike was called for 17 August. The walkout in Roslyn was part of a greater movement throughout the United States during the 1880s to strengthen organized labor, and for this reason management viewed it with alarm. Rather than negotiating, the Northern Pacific attempted instead to break both the strike and the Knights of Labor. Within a week a trainload of black miners from Illinois arrived under the protection of heavily armed guards.

The company's dramatic show of power produced both intended and unintended results. In the short run, the railroad accomplished its goal of crushing organized labor in Roslyn. During the first tense days the company braced for violence that appeared imminent but did not erupt. It then introduced its new workforce into the mines.

But while the harvest of Roslyn coal resumed, challenges to the company arose from unexpected quarters. Prompted by press accounts of the arrival of United States "deputy marshals," the governor of Washington Territory launched an investigation that resulted in the arrest of the company's guards and official condemnation of the company's paramilitary practices.[7]

Subsequent events demonstrate that Governor Eugene Semple's major interest in the Roslyn affair centered on two constitutional issues. The first involved the separation of powers between federal and local governments, the second the legitimacy of private corporations fielding armed militias. These questions concerned him quite apart from any interest he had in the labor dispute over wages and hours in Roslyn coal mines.

On the day that he learned of the arrival in his territory of "a body of men calling themselves 'detectives,' who were regularly armed and uniformed and acting under officers with military titles," Governor Semple asked the Kittitas County sheriff to "ascertain by what authority they claim to act" and to inform him immediately. He also contacted his attorney-general in Seattle, asking for an opinion concerning the line of demarcation between the authority of the sheriff and that of the United States marshal in the territory.

Two days later Sheriff Packwood reported from Ellensburg that "there are about forty armed men, deputy United States marshals, and about fifty negroes in coal mine No. 3. They are guarding the negroes. The miners at camps Nos. 1 and 2 say they are working for less wages and on the eleven-hour system, and that it will, in the event of their

The Number 3 mine in Ronald is photographed at the approach of winter.
Photograph courtesy of the Roslyn Museum.

A winter scene shows Ronald and the Cascade Mountains under a thick blanket of snow.
Photograph courtesy of the Roslyn Museum.

being allowed to work, bring them to the same system of work and wages, and they say they shan't work."

He continued by reporting that the guards had forcibly established a camp on land claimed by a resident named Ross, and that the latter had filed complaints with the local justice of the peace. In consequence the sheriff "arrested the whole posse" and placed them under his custody on 22 August. Sheriff Packwood observed that "there is bitter feeling against the negroes and United States marshals among the miners, and I fear there will be bloodshed over the matter," but concluded that he felt he could keep peace in the area.

By 27 August Governor Semple had heard from Attorney-General Metcalfe, who informed him that neither the United States attorney nor the United States marshal at Seattle had authorized the deputizing of marshals in Roslyn and knew of no justification to do so. The attorney-general then expressed the opinion that "if detectives in the employ of private corporations are deputized as United States deputy marshals for the purpose of being used in the interest

of such corporations, such an act, in my judgment, is reprehensible, dangerous to our liberties, and censurable in the highest degree."

In response to these reports, Governor Semple telegraphed the sheriff of Kittitas County that the "armed body of men calling themselves 'detectives,' and who are reportedly fortifying themselves at Roslyn, have no authority as United States deputy marshals. The presence of such an armed body of men from another jurisdiction upon our soil, in the employ of a corporation or a private party, is a reflection upon the law-abiding people of Kittitas County, and an offense against the sovereignty of Washington Territory. I trust that you will use the full power of your county to uphold the laws and the dignity of this commonwealth, and that if there is a probability that you will be confronted with difficulties which you can not overcome, you will promptly appeal to this office."

In reply to this telegram, Sheriff Packwood invited Governor Semple to visit Roslyn in person, an invitation which he immediately accepted. He arrived in Cle Elum on the morning of 29 August, accompanied by Lt. Col. Hicks of his staff and the territory's attorney-general. There he joined the sheriff and H. J. Snively, Kittitas County prosecuting attorney. The governor's party then toured the controversial site outside the Number 3 mine where the Northern Pacific had set up a camp for the black miners and defensive works for the guards.

In a subsequent report to the Secretary of the Interior, Governor Semple summarized the findings of Kittitas County prosecuting attorney Snively, who found evidence that the guards had "exhibited weapons in threatening manners" during their original passage through Roslyn, "with guns at the windows of each of the said cars [of the train carrying the black miners] aimed at a large

A crowd gathers in front of the Roslyn Bottling Works around the turn of the century.
Photograph courtesy of the Roslyn Museum.

crowd of people standing in the vicinity of the depot." Snively found that "these armed men acted in a very insulting manner towards the citizens of Roslyn," and detailed the accusations of Alexander Ross against the guards who detained him in a boxcar after entering onto land that he claimed as his.

In his report to the Interior Secretary, Governor Semple stated his conclusions in the following manner:

"The bringing into the Territory of these contract laborers would, *it was supposed*, give offense to the white miners at Roslyn; they, *it was supposed*, would desire to attack the negroes; and the lawful authorities, *it was supposed*, would fail or refuse to do their duty. Upon this string of suppositions the managers of the coal mines relied to justify their action in ordering this invasion of Washington Territory.

"My investigations convinced me that none of these suppositions had any foundation in fact except the first one.

"The people of Roslyn, I am convinced, are law-abiding and intelligent, and I had an exceptionally favorable opportunity for observing their physiognomies, for they turned out en masse when I reached their town, and my conveyance was driven between double lines of men that evidently included nearly the entire number of the miners at that point. I looked these men in the face, and they appeared to be sober and intelligent. They treated my party with the utmost respect, although they were sorely disappointed when I was compelled to inform them that they had misapprehended the object of my visit, and that my office had no authority to undertake the adjustment of differences between them and the coal companies.

A Fourth of July parade progresses down Pennsylvania Avenue in 1901.
Photograph courtesy of the Roslyn Museum.

This parade in Roslyn in 1899 drew crowds of participants as well as spectators.
Photograph courtesy of the Roslyn Museum.

"Again, the people of Kittitas County are law-abiding and patriotic, and their officers are honorable and courageous men, who would not, in my opinion, fail to do their duty under any circumstances.

"The conclusion, therefore, must be made that the bringing of these 'detectives' to mine No. 3 was an unjustifiable proceeding on the part of the coal mine owners, and I think may be properly characterized as an outrage. I gave this as my opinion to the attorneys and agents of the companies, and stated to them, that even if, as they claimed, there was no law by which such proceedings could be prevented or punished, that I proposed to urge the local authorities to take some action and let the report show that they had not submitted to the outrage tamely.

"Hon. H. J. Snively, the prosecuting attorney for the district including Kittitas County, came to Cle Elum while my party was there, and I requested him to use such efforts as might appear to him to be authorized by law to disperse the 'detectives,' who were intrenched at mine No. 3. He informed me that he had made arrangements to do so, and that if they decided to remain there he would have them arrested on preliminary process, but that if they disbanded within a reasonable time he would take no action until he could lay the matter before the grand jury.

"I have made an extended report of this matter because I believe it is one of great importance. The system by which corporations or rich individuals claim the right to maintain a standing armed force to overcome opposition to their schemes is one that has grown up within the last twenty years, and constitutes a serious menace to our free institutions. These so-called 'detective agencies' are almost exactly on a par with the societies of 'High Binders' amongst the Chinese, mere organized bodies of ruffians, offering, for hire, to become the instruments of the rich and strong for the oppression of the poor and weak. Not being able to show any authority of law for their existence, they and their employers point to a line of precedents beginning in the most corrupt period in the history of the Republic, when the idea of liberty was as completely subordinated to the idea of material wealth as it was under the Doges of Venice. The action of this office is in a new line of precedents, and I have recommended to the Code com-

missioners of this Territory that they incorporate in their report to the legislature a statute that will enable its officers to effectively deal with such cases as the one herein mentioned."

The actions of county authorities and the visit to Roslyn of Governor Semple preceded by one day a special poll of miners on 30 August. In this election a majority of miners agreed to return to work. The major issues had still not been addressed by the company, however, and the following day a number of miners petitioned the governor to help them obtain better schooling, an eight-hour day, increased mine safety, and higher wages. Unfortunately for the miners, the governor claimed no influence over these matters.

Although the results of the election on 30 August were reported by some newspapers as a "settlement" of the strike, the referen-

The Cle Elum Livery was located behind city hall on 3rd and Pennsylvania.
Photograph courtesy of Albert Schober.

dum did not satisfy militant members of the Knights of Labor. Many white miners in Roslyn believed that the black strikebreakers' votes had decided the election in favor of the company. Resentment against the strikebreakers mounted, and accusations of importing votes to decide labor elections echoed in the press.

On 7 September, a week after the back-to-work agreement, Roslyn's white miners threatened to strike again if the company refused to recognize either the Knights of Labor or the Miners' Union. The company refused, and another strike was called that stopped production in all mines and halted all but mail trains on the Roslyn branch line. In response the company paid off those who had been working and closed down its Roslyn coal operations, while the company's black miners in Ronald continued development of the company's Number 3 mine.

The striking workers yielded by the end of September, their resolve weakened by the onset of cold weather and the company's steadfastness. The company imposed wage reductions and layoffs, and refused to dismiss its black miners. This new "agreement" gave jobs to only about one half of the striking miners, with preference given to married men.

The Northern Pacific's decision to challenge its striking miners with imported black workers from Illinois was consistent with the general trend in labor-management relations during the last quarter of the nineteenth century. This was a period when little or no legislation governed relations between corporate enterprises and their workers, and when labor unions struggled for—among other things—the right to exist.

At the same time, the nature of Governor Semple's response reflected a growing concern by government leaders and others over the power of large corporations. This sentiment led the framers of the state constitu-

tion in 1889 to specify, in the section which guaranteed the right of individuals to bear arms in order to protect themselves or the state, that nothing in that section should be construed as authorizing "individuals or corporations to organize, maintain, or employ an armed body of men."[8]

Labor relations remained tense in Roslyn during the winter of 1888–89, as the railroad continued to bring black miners from the Midwest to Roslyn. Increasingly the new arrivals, who came with their families, began to replace some of the tough, single men whom the company had selected to fill the unenviable role of strikebreaker. Such a worker would earn the opprobrium of union members under any circumstances, but the problem in Roslyn was intensified by racial differences. The result in Roslyn was the infliction of social wounds that took decades to heal.

While blacks sometimes became a focus

Two youths wearing knickers ride a mule in Roslyn in the early 1900s.

Photograph courtesy of the Local History Collection, Ellensburg Public Library.

for labor strife, such as in two short strikes by Roslyn mule drivers in December 1888 and January 1889, the white miners' major complaints remained wages and working conditions. As a result, most dissatisfaction was directed toward the Northern Pacific's management personnel. Accusations of cheating men at the company store found expression in the Seattle *Post-Intelligencer* in its edition of 25 December 1888, and the intensity of some miners' hostility was revealed in assaults against managers and the discharge of firearms. In one extreme example, mine superintendent Alexander

Ronald was bound and left on the railroad tracks, and only escaped death when a railroad brakeman pulled him quickly to safety.

Social tension abated gradually after February 1889 when more than two hundred white miners left Roslyn. Those who remained accepted both the company's working conditions and the fact of the black miners' presence. Interracial relations still left much to be desired, but open hostility remained exceptional. Instead, discrimination took such forms as excluding blacks from the city cemetery. A year after the

A funeral procession makes its way to Roslyn's cemeteries with victims from the 1892 explosion.
Photograph courtesy of the Roslyn Museum.

Portrait of a distinguished Roslynite.
Photograph courtesy of the Local History Collection, Ellensburg Public Library.

disastrous mine explosion of 1892, the city council addressed the cemetery issue by suggesting that the Northern Pacific grant separate deeds of donation, one for the "City Cemetery," and another for land that black Roslynites soon consecrated as the "Mount Olivet" cemetery.

Although it was not easy for blacks in America to win acceptance and live harmoniously with whites during the late nine-

A snow bucking outfit negotiates a trestle over Mosquito Creek in 1887.
Photograph courtesy of the Yakima Valley Museum & Historical Association. (Gibson album).

teenth century, the circumstances of the black miners' introduction into Roslyn made integration—or even peaceful coexistence—especially difficult. Because they came as strikebreakers, their continued employment provided a continual reminder to white union members of previous defeats in labor negotiations with the company. Incidents of violence were rare, but some did occur—such as the barroom homicide in Roslyn of a black whose persistence in song had irritated some white patrons.

For many black miners, however, employment in Roslyn brought with it a social status unlike any they had experienced before. For though the community of white miners was hostile, the area's economic and political kingpin—the railroad—supported them. The personal protection offered by the company's armed guards was in one sense dignifying. And, as long as black miners worked alongside whites, the earning power of both remained comparable, a situation that was unusual in American industry until well after the civil rights reforms of the 1960s.

Certainly it was not the Northern Pacific's intention to advance the civil rights of blacks or to engage in social engineering in Roslyn. The company's purpose clearly was to break the white miners' strike, to avoid recognizing the Knights of Labor, and to wring wage concessions from its employees. In this it was successful. But at the same time the company contributed significantly to the immigration of blacks to Washington state, many with their families. The descendants of nearly all of these individuals now live elsewhere in Washington and throughout the United States, but many return to Roslyn annually to honor the memory of family roots that reach back nearly one hundred years.

CHAPTER 5

Immigrant Stew

As a result of the labor strife of 1888 and 1889, a significant number of miners who had come to Roslyn at the first call of the Northern Pacific Railway left the region for what they hoped would be better opportunities elsewhere. Those who remained were quieter men, often with families, who during the next decade helped to define the character of the community as it completed its transformation from temporary mining camp to permanent town. During this same period Cle Elum established itself as an independent community, and laid the bases for its substantial growth in the first decade of the twentieth century.

By 1890 coal mining had transformed Roslyn into a bustling community of 1,481 people. After a fire destroyed much of the downtown business section in June 1888, Roslyn rebuilt its commercial center in the western frontier style that its main street still preserves today. The company store at the corner of First and Pennsylvania, completed in 1889, provided the town's commercial anchor. The same year the Brick Tavern opened for business diagonally opposite. A com-

The Roslyn N.W.I. store (on facing page) was listed on the National Register of Historic Structures in April 1973.
Photograph courtesy of the Roslyn Museum.

The Roslyn N.W.I. store was stacked with goods for this photo in 1919.
Photograph courtesy of the Roslyn Museum.

This is a view of "Coxey's Army," waiting for the train to depart Yakima in 1894.
Photograph courtesy of the Yakima Valley Museum & Historical Association.

pany hotel stood as another reminder of the railroad's economic control over the town. Future growth, however, would lighten the shadow cast by the Northern Pacific, as merchants and businessmen flocked to Roslyn to serve the needs of a growing population.

The first few years of the 1890s tested the resolve of many Roslynites, as the community weathered the effects of a severe economic downturn, a disastrous mine explosion, recurrent labor discontent, and the collapse of the local bank. Shipments of Roslyn coal dipped during 1891 as the result of a lost contract with the Union Pacific Railroad, and contributed to the loss of full employment for Roslyn miners. More serious was a mine explosion, caused by deficient ventilation, that claimed forty-five lives in May 1892. Immediately a relief committee formed that collected $7,000 from outside Roslyn and more than $2,000 from within. The money was distributed to sur-

viving widows and orphans, who later received additional sums of money in settlement of liability claims against the Northern Pacific.

The failure of the Ben Snipes and Company Bank in 1893 occurred approximately nine months after a gang of western-style outlaws relieved the bank of $5,000 worth of deposits. The bank's closure came during a cyclical downturn of the nation's financial markets. This "panic" was brought on, economic historians think, by overinvestment in capital goods relative to the ability of consumers to purchase products. The result was deflation of prices and wages that took their greatest toll on factory, farm, and mine workers.

During this period of economic hardship, the Populist Party gained considerable strength among farmers and laborers alike. Kittitas County residents showed support for this movement during May 1894 when more than one thousand unemployed workers, inspired by a national leader named Jacob Coxey, marched through the area to petition Congress for reform. In a show of solidarity, Ellensburg merchants and farmers donated food and other provisions to this contingent of "Coxey's Army." A few weeks later effects of the strike against the Pullman Company in Illinois reached the Kittitas Valley, as railroad workers abandoned trains in sympathy, halting virtually all traffic.

During this time of national social unrest, a labor dispute again interrupted Roslyn coal production. Miners left their jobs when the company proposed to restore to the men five days' work, but at twenty percent lower wages. The nation was mired in recession, demand for coal was slack, and the company hoped that the miners' desire to work more than two days per week would induce them to accept a substantial hourly wage cut. For more than three months the miners held fast, until the company threatened to resume production with new miners. After two ballots, a majority finally acceded to the new conditions, and Roslyn miners returned to work.

For miners, as for farmers, difficult times continued during the mid nineties. Kittitas County shared this fate with much of the state as well as the nation. The first glimpses of a reversal of fortune were seen at what appeared to be the worst of times, in 1894. During that year a small gold rush brought hundreds of miners and prospectors to the hills that were drained by the Swauk and Cle Elum rivers. Enough gold was found to encourage the establishment of a serious mining industry, and for two decades the Mt. Stuart range was alive with activity.

The year 1894 also brought the establishment of the Cle Elum Coal Company, an independent operation that mined coal on land leased from Judge Thomas Gamble.

Production remained modest until the Northwestern Improvement Company purchased and expanded this operation six years later, but the mine gave Cle Elum a start on what later became the city's major industry.

In 1897 increased demand for coal and higher prices finally brought the long-awaited upturn to the Washington coal industry. Roslyn returned to full employment,

A European tradition in dress is shown in this photograph of the Central Baths in Cle Elum.
Photograph courtesy of Albert Schober.

Twenty-four different nationalities are represented in this photograph of Roslyn school children.
Photograph courtesy of the Roslyn Museum.

and then its population surged as the annual output of coal rose from less than 300,000 tons to nearly 900,000 tons by 1900. Housing strained to meet the new demand, although construction added 150 new residences during the building season of 1899. By the time census takers had completed their count in 1900, Roslyn's population stood at 2,783, nearly double its 1890 figure, with most newcomers arriving in the decade's last three years. Cle Elum also participated in this boom, with its 1890 population more than doubled to 762. However, results from the 1900 census tell us much more about Roslyn and Cle Elum than simple population totals.

The Demography of
Roslyn, Ronald, and Cle Elum in 1900

The Roslyn coal field attracted men from coal mining regions in other parts of the United States and from nations with well developed coal industries. The first miners in Roslyn were predominantly of English ancestry. As the mining industry grew, these men performed many of the skilled jobs and occupied a disproportionate number of supervisory positions. First-generation Italian immigrants initially supplied a large proportion of unskilled labor. Then, during the 1890s, and particularly during the latter years of that decade, a growing number of Slavic immigrants (many of whom are identified in census records as "Austrians") swelled the unskilled labor pool and added to the area's ethnic mix.

Census statistics from the year 1900 and other evidence provide some clues to the social characteristics of Roslyn and Cle Elum at the turn of the century. The two communities differed in population, in economic composition, and in social structure. Roslyn, the larger of the two towns, was a community where two out of three males aged fourteen or older worked in or around a coal mine. Cle Elum, on the other hand, was a railroad junction, a hub for the agricultural activity of the upper Kittitas

Valley, and an entertainment center for loggers and miners. In 1900 its coal mine provided only 72 jobs compared to Roslyn's 823, and accounted for less than a fifth of the occupations of Cle Elum's adult males. Expressed another way, while Roslyn's economy in 1900 was several times larger, Cle Elum's was already more diverse.

In social terms, Roslyn had larger numbers and a different variety of races, nationalities, and ethnic groups. Twenty-two percent of Roslyn's population was black in the year 1900, and fully forty percent of Roslyn's population in 1900 was foreign born. The foreign country of origin claimed by the greatest number of Roslyn residents in 1900 was England. This country claimed 283 native sons among Roslynites, followed by Austria with 210, Italy with 189, Germany with 88, Scotland with 80, and Wales with 52. Immigrants from fourteen other countries added another 201 foreign born persons to the total population. These included

36 Canadians, 32 Russians, and 31 Swedes among the larger contingents, and 1 Czech, 2 Asian Indians, and 3 Belgians among the smaller.

Cle Elum presented nearly as much diversity in its smaller Tower of Babel. Italians formed the largest block of foreign born, with forty-three natives. The English trailed with thirty-four, followed by twenty-nine Germans, twenty-one Canadians, and twelve Welshmen. Austrians and Irishmen each accounted for ten natives, and forty persons from twelve other countries completed the count. In Cle Elum, only twenty-six percent of residents were foreign born, a significantly smaller proportion than in Roslyn. Another difference from Roslyn was the almost total absence of blacks (the census takers counted only one in Cle Elum compared to 623 in Roslyn). Finally, Cle Elum claimed the only remnants of the once numerous Chinese born population (reduced to seven in 1900).

This photo shows the Roman Catholic Church in Cle Elum, before its destruction in the fire of 1918.
Photograph courtesy of Albert Schober.

In 1900 the population of Ronald was 345, almost half that of Cle Elum and nearly double its 1970 census. The census profile of the residents of Ronald resembled Roslyn's more closely than Cle Elum's. Almost one third of the population was black, and another third was foreign born. As in Roslyn, the largest contingent of foreign born was comprised of Englishmen, who accounted for thirty-seven persons. Italians were second with twenty-three, followed by Scots with thirteen, Germans with eleven, and Canadians and Irish with eight each. There were also seven Austrians, six Swedes, and half a dozen others from Hungary, Poland, Russia, and Wales.

Considering the aggregate populations of Roslyn, Ronald, and Cle Elum, the census of 1900 reveals that the immigration patterns into the upper Kittitas Valley diverged significantly from the general trend of immigration into Washington state. In the state as a whole, for example, Italians in 1900 ranked as only the ninth largest immigrant group. By comparison, in Roslyn, Ronald, and Cle Elum, Italians were the second largest immigrant group. Similarly, the "Austrian" contingent (probably comprised mostly of Slavs whose native country is now Yugoslavia) accounted for only 2.1% of the population statewide, but almost 16% in Roslyn, Ronald, and Cle Elum. The proportion of English, Scots, and Welsh in Roslyn, Ronald, and Cle Elum also far exceeded the average for the state, while immigrants from both Canada and northern Europe (Germany and Scandinavia) were underrepresented.

The special mix of first-generation immigrants in Roslyn and Cle Elum had much

These members of the Polish National Alliance were photographed in Cle Elum circa 1915.
Photograph courtesy of Albert Schober.

to do with changing national trends. From 1860 to 1890 most immigrants to the United States came from northern Europe, especially from Germany and from Scandinavia. Toward the end of the century, however, when Roslyn and Cle Elum received their greatest influxes of population, emigration patterns shifted to southern Europe, especially to Italy and the Slavic portions of the Austro-Hungarian empire.

From the national perspective, the new immigrants from southern and eastern

Members of Roslyn's Silvio Pellico Lodge all hold beer bottles in this photo from 1912. A lodge receipt (below) is printed in Italian.
Photograph courtesy of the Roslyn Museum.

Russian Orthodox priests are photographed in 1916 at their church in Cle Elum.
Photograph courtesy of Albert Schober.

Europe represented only a small portion of the more than ten million persons of foreign birth who were counted as U.S. residents in 1900. But gathered in large concentrations, they imparted a distinct character to the coal mining communities of the upper Kittitas Valley.

It would be a mistake, however, to describe Roslyn or Cle Elum as a "melting pot"

of races and cultures. In Roslyn in particular the very diversity of ethnic backgrounds and the often shallow roots in America of the European emigrants fostered the maintenance of strong "microcommunity" ties among individuals of a common culture or language. As a result ethnic self-help associations and fraternal organizations flourished in Roslyn, and contributed to preserving the separate identities of numerous immigrant groups.

Later, a number of forces combined to mute the chorus of distinct linguistic and national voices. One factor was a near hysteric and decidedly xenophobic patriotism whipped up by government propaganda during World War I. Another was the effect upon second-generation immigrants of a common English language education. And a third was a stanched flow of new immigrants, especially as Roslyn and Cle Elum began to decline in population after World War I. To this day the evidence of a polycultural heritage for Roslyn is visible in the city's twenty-two separate cemetery plots and in the frequency of non–Anglo-Saxon names in the Roslyn telephone book.

In addition to recording the birthplaces of first-generation immigrants, the census of 1900 also listed the state of birth of residents born in the United States. Washington was the single most cited state, but it may be

safely assumed that a high proportion of these natives were children. In 1900 Roslyn boasted a total of 697 children aged under ten, and this group probably accounted for most of the 575 Roslyn residents who were born in Washington.

Cle Elum's contingent of Washington born differs somewhat from Roslyn's. In Cle Elum the census takers counted 177 Washington born residents and only 159 children under ten. These numbers indicate that a score or more of Cle Elum's Washington born residents came to Kittitas County as adults or that their parents were established in Cle Elum prior to 1890.

In ranking the states of origins of Roslyn and Cle Elum residents, one finds both coincidences and differences. After Washington, three of the leading four states of origin—Illinois, Pennsylvania, and Missouri—are the same. This fact indicates that both whites and blacks emigrated from midwestern coal states, since Roslyn's U.S. born population was nearly half black, and Cle Elum's was virtually all white. Illinois ranked second after Washington in both communities, claiming almost 6.5% of the residents in Roslyn and nearly 6% in Cle Elum. In Roslyn the number three, four, and five states were Pennsylvania, Virginia, and Missouri; whereas in Cle Elum Missouri, Pennsylvania, and Minnesota occupied these spots.

The bottom half of the lists were less similar. Each community had two unique states on its list, and where the states were the same, the rank order was different. States six through ten on Roslyn's list were Ohio, Wisconsin, Kansas, Michigan, and Kentucky. On Cle Elum's list, the same ranked states were Indiana, Kentucky, Oregon, Kansas, and Ohio. In Ronald, the rank order of states of origin coincided with neither that of Roslyn nor Cle Elum. After Washington, its top six states were Missouri,

The Public Meat Market in Roslyn had a cashier's booth in 1923.
Photograph courtesy of the Roslyn Museum.

Virginia, Pennsylvania, Illinois, Oregon, and Minnesota.

In all three communities, the populations were comprised of a higher than average number of males—fifty-nine percent in Roslyn, sixty-three percent in Ronald, and sixty-one percent in Cle Elum. This compared to a national average of fifty-one percent in 1900. Although the proportion of married persons to singles was about average in the three communities, the age distribution was skewed in favor of individuals in their prime working years (25–34 years). This means that among adults, the number of single males was higher in Roslyn, Ronald, and Cle Elum than in the population as a whole. Not surprisingly, none of the communities had many elderly residents.

In addition to population statistics, the 1900 census provides interesting data on the occupations of community residents. In Roslyn, coal mining was the major source of employment, but the sheer size of the town attracted other businesses as well. After coal mining (823 persons) and general

The Roslyn Bakery sold produce and canned food in addition to dry goods in 1919.
Photograph courtesy of the Roslyn Museum.

Scotty and Charles Hugg occupy the front room of Zentner's Cigar Store in Cle Elum.
Photograph courtesy of Albert Schober.

labor (sixty persons, some of whom may have worked for coal operators), the next largest occupational classifications were mechanical trades and crafts (fifty persons), domestic services (fifty-four persons), and construction and building related occupations (thirty-three persons). An equal number of individuals (twenty-seven) were employed in either food service jobs or in the alcoholic beverage industry (as bartenders or brewery workers). Another twenty-three sold, manufactured, or repaired clothing and related articles, and nineteen individuals engaged in retail trade. There were eighteen persons providing personal services, thirteen educators, eight government employees, six each of clergy and professionals, and five physicians.

Pictured inside the Zentner Cigar Factory in 1905 are (left to right) Fred Zentner, George Hugg, Charles Hugg, and Guy Van Fleet.
Photograph courtesy of Albert Schober.

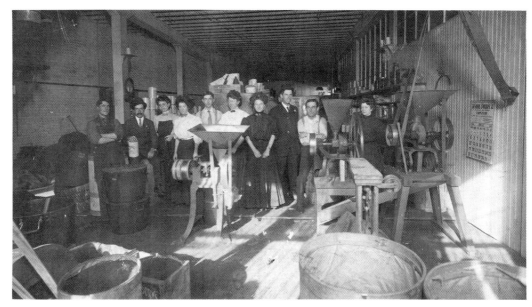

The workforce of the Zentner Cigar Factory poses for this photo circa 1905.
Photograph courtesy of Albert Schober.

Cle Elum's occupational picture differed somewhat from Roslyn's. Far fewer of its residents engaged in retail trade (only one in general wares and two in clothing) or engaged in mechanical trades and crafts (ten). On the other hand, Cle Elum provided residents with eighteen railroad related jobs compared to only five in Roslyn and Ronald. More loggers or woodcutters were counted in Cle Elum than in Roslyn, and the town also had proportionally more people engaged in the sawmill, construction, and building trades (nineteen in Cle Elum, thirty-three in Roslyn). Cle Elum had the area's only cigar maker, and a number of boarding houses and inns. There were ten bartenders in Cle Elum (a larger per capita number than in Roslyn), and one professed prostitute. In addition, the Cle Elum census area included sixty-three farmers compared to only five in Roslyn.

By far the largest occupation in Ronald was coal mining, which employed seventy-four persons or almost half the adult males. Thirty-eight men, representing one quarter

Perched on the roof of the the Depot Bar in Cle Elum is an early Foster and Kleiser billboard for Olympia Beer.
Photograph courtesy of Albert Schober.

Friends and well-wishers of the Owl Saloon stand on an early Cle Elum boardwalk.
Photograph courtesy of Albert Schober.

It was a tall step up to the second floor door of the Pacific Bar in Cle Elum.
Photograph courtesy of Albert Schober.

A potbellied stove warms the inside of the Torino Saloon in Roslyn in 1912.
Photograph courtesy of the Roslyn Museum.

of all adult males, worked the quartz veins or placer mines of the surrounding region and were also counted as inhabitants of Ronald. This compared to only sixteen hard rock miners each in Roslyn and Cle Elum. Others included in the Ronald census were eleven farmers and a sprinkling of wood-

cutters, construction trades workers, mechanics, and craftsmen.

The 1900 census did not list an occupation for most women living in Roslyn, Ronald, and Cle Elum. Two Roslyn women indicated to the census takers that they worked at sewing in their homes. But in general, unpaid domestic work and child raising appears to have been the nearly universal occupation of married women. As for children, 541 in Roslyn attended school, mostly from age six to fourteen. The Cle Elum schools retained children in the classroom slightly longer. The census indicated that 154 Cle Elum children attended school, including at least a dozen of the 75 children aged fifteen to nineteen.

At this period in U.S. history it was normal for children to begin working at age fourteen or younger. For a child to complete the eighth grade was an accomplishment—one which the schools recognized with "graduation" certificates. Many states, in-

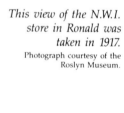

George Robinson received this certificate upon graduation from the eighth grade in 1917.
Photograph courtesy of the Roslyn Museum.

Rapid Growth, 1900–1915

Both Roslyn and Cle Elum had grown rapidly in the closing years of the nineteenth century. Their populations would grow even faster still in the first decade of the twentieth century, and reach peaks around 1915. Change came fastest to Cle Elum, where the

cluding Washington, had yet to enact child labor legislation, and it was not unusual for boys to work at such jobs as picking coal for six ten-hour days per week.

The census statistics for 1900 reveal that an interesting mosaic of races, nationalities, and vocations constituted the communities of Roslyn, Ronald, and Cle Elum at the turn of the century. For the most part these disparate elements worked harmoniously alongside each other, keeping in mind both the common good and the welfare of one's family and friends.

This view of the N.W.I. store in Ronald was taken in 1917.
Photograph courtesy of the Roslyn Museum.

A special occasion drew crowds to Cle Elum's First Street in the summer of 1909.
Photograph courtesy of Albert Schober.

population surged to an estimated 3,200 by 1912. Growth came for three reasons. First, the coal mining industry became truly significant in Cle Elum once the Northwestern Improvement Company extended its operations to the Cle Elum end of the field. Second, Cle Elum benefited when the Cascade Lumber Company increased its logging operations in the nearby Teanaway drainage. Third, the community served as a center for commerce and operational headquarters for both the hard rock mining activity that entered a corporate phase of operation, and for the public works and railroad projects that reached a crescendo of activity in the years from 1909 to 1915.

A symbolic step in the coming to age of Cle Elum was taken in 1902 when the residents voted to incorporate as a city. Thomas Gamble, the highly respected pioneer judge, became the city's first mayor. At about the same time, Cle Elum and

Roslyn entered the era of electricity following construction by the N.W.I. of local power generating plants. Another sign of maturity was the construction of a new, two-story public school in 1902.

During the early years of the century's first decade, much of the impetus for the growth of Cle Elum came from the Northern Pacific Railway. In a pamphlet entitled "Opportunities—Openings for Business Locations on the Line of the Northern Pacific Railway," the railroad's "general emigration agent" advertised openings in "Clealum" for both a bank and a flour mill. These needs reflected the city's growing role as a business center for the upper Kittitas Valley, and the importance of agriculture in the region. (The Northern Pacific, citing difficulties in telegraphy, waged a losing battle in the early twentieth century to revise the official spelling of Cle Elum's name.) One result of this promotion of Cle Elum was the founding by

This electrified Milwaukee Road passenger train was photographed west of Cle Elum in 1920.

Photograph courtesy of the Washington State Historical Society. Photo by Asahel Curtis.

The Milwaukee Road constructed this substation near the depot in South Cle Elum following electrification of the line.
Photograph courtesy of the Washington State Historical Society. Photo by Asahel Curtis.

Frank Carpenter of the Cle Elum State Bank in 1904.

The existence of mineral in the mountains north of Cle Elum touched off a minor gold rush in the 1890s and a small wave of commercial mining activity a decade later. When a Seattle corporation decided to increase its scale of operations in the Cle Elum mining district, it made Cle Elum its local headquarters. The first phase of this project involved constructing a railway to transport mineral to Cle Elum from the mine sites. In 1909 U.S. and French capitalists organized the Kittitas Railway and Power Company, which soon began to acquire and grade a right-of-way. The company also built what was to become a depot at Salmon La Sac. But the impending outbreak of World War I caused the French financiers to withdraw, and the structure became a U.S. Forest Service guard station instead. Work on the railway ceased, and mining operations on a commercial scale never materialized.

During the first decade of the twentieth century, increasing activity in transportation and agriculture affected areas outside the limits of Walter Reed's townsite. On the other side of the Yakima River, the town of South Cle Elum received a large boost when locating engineers for the Chicago, Milwaukee, St. Paul and Pacific Railroad surveyed their new right-of-way through the town in 1906. The townsite had been platted in 1891 by S. T. Packwood, president of the "Cle Elum Land and Development Company," in the same year that M. C. Miller established a lumber mill there. However, significant development of the town awaited the beginning of tracklaying and then tunnel construction that occupied workers to 1909 and beyond.

Along with the railroad, new residential structures sprouted in South Cle Elum, which a journalist described in 1910 as "practically a new town." The Milwaukee Road made South Cle Elum a division point on its transcontinental route, and later established a substation there following elec-

A construction crew worked on the High Line irrigation ditch at Nelson Siding circa 1912.
Photograph courtesy of the Roslyn Museum.

trification of the line. Of lesser immediate impact was the completion of the Snoqualmie Pass highway in 1913. This project gave a small boost to the local economy during its years of construction, but provided an immense source of future commercial activity.

In agriculture the most important event of the second decade of the twentieth century was the construction of the high-line canal by the federal government. On 1 December 1912 a writer for the *Seattle Times* described this project as "the largest irrigation proposition yet undertaken by the government." Total cost of the project was $5 million, to be repaid by bonds issued by the affected irrigation district. "The government," the writer stated, "has already completed its dam at Lake Kachess and as this brings the remaining 10,000 or 12,000 acres of the tributary lands around Cle Elum under irrigation, the horticultural and agricultural outlook was never before so bright, as they are adapted to subdivision into small farming tracts that are capable of intensive cultivation." Land values rose appreciably during the teens, as farmers enjoyed good prices and strong demand through the end of World War I.

A Sense of Community

Despite a significant diversity of backgrounds, the residents of Roslyn and Cle Elum were drawn together by experiencing common adversity and by sharing an interest in community betterment. Everyone benefited when the community united to

This is a photograph of the original Lake Cle Elum reclamation dam.
Photograph courtesy of Albert Schober.

fight fires, provide for clean drinking water, and aid victims of disasters. Roslyn residents fought their community's first major fire with a bucket brigade during 1888, and subsequently established a volunteer fire department. During 1890 the Roslyn city council purchased both fire hose and a three-hundred-pound bell.

Cle Elum remained without a formal volunteer fire department until after incorporation in 1902, although fire had destroyed a considerable portion of the business district in 1891. The city's worst disaster ever occurred in 1918 when a fire, whipped by high winds, consumed a thirty

Cle Elum residents removed belongings from their homes as the fire of 1918 advanced uncontrolled.
Photograph courtesy of Albert Schober.

The photographs at left document the destructive power of the fire that consumed a large portion of Cle Elum in 1918.
Photograph courtesy of Albert Schober.

This photo shows the rebuilt, fireproof hospital that was erected on the foundations of the original structure that burned in 1908.
Photograph courtesy of Albert Schober.

square block area from downtown east for a distance of ten blocks. The fire left fifteen hundred persons homeless and caused a financial loss of more than one million dollars.

In both Roslyn and Cle Elum, natural disasters elicited generous community responses. Roslyn city council minutes contain numerous references to donations of financial aid for the victims of the Ellensburg fire of 1889, the mine explosion survivers in 1892, and earthquake victims in San Francisco and Italy in 1906 and 1909. After the fire of 1918 in Cle Elum, members of both communities mobilized to assist the homeless.

An additional example of mutual self-help was the construction of the Cle Elum–Roslyn Beneficial Association Hospital. This facility was constructed in 1905 and operated with dues paid by miners and health shares purchased by persons not employed in the mines. Unfortunately, the hospital burned to the ground in 1908 after a small fire began in one corner of the structure. Although promptly discovered, the fire could not be quickly extinguished due to the hospital's secluded location and lack of pressurized water. Within two days of this disaster, the residents of Roslyn and Cle Elum and of-

ficials of the Northwestern Improvement Company formulated plans to rebuild the hospital. An N.W.I. architect quickly drafted plans for a fire resistant structure that builders raised within eight months on the old foundations.

The N.W.I. under the local management of B. F. Bush also contributed to the founding of a Y.M.C.A. in Roslyn. In the fall of 1902, Bush offered to finance the construction of "an attractive, moral place of recreation" for young men in Roslyn if they would form an association, take charge of the building, and repay his interest-free loan as soon as possible. The men accepted Bush's offer, and a two-story building on First Street was erected that contained a bowling alley, gymnasium, meeting rooms, and lockers where miners could hang wet work clothes. The association soon became a focal point for community affairs where adult English classes were conducted for foreign immigrants and self-improvement courses in subjects like mechanical drawing and electricity were offered.

Since its earliest days, Roslyn has exuded a special charm. One early description of the town appeared in the Seattle *Post-Intelligencer* on 7 April 1899. The paper's "special correspondent" compared Roslyn favorably to other towns of its type: "The traveler who visits Roslyn for the first time will be surprised to find, instead of the ordinary Pacific coast coal hamlet, a city of about 3,000 inhabitants with splendid business houses and many elegant residences." A still favorable, but somewhat less exultant appraisal, was offered a little more than a dozen years later by a professor of mining engineering at the University of Washington. He observed around 1913 that "living conditions are better than in many of the coal camps of the country."[1]

Community spirit in Roslyn received a boost in 1913 when the Northwestern Improvement Company decided to sell the leased land on which residents' homes were constructed. The decision won the approval of the *Cascade Miner,* which anticipated that Roslyn residents would maintain their homes better with full ownership. "The hundreds of homes in Roslyn that are surrounded with little grass plots and flower beds are witnesses to the pride which some of the residents take in their homes. Their number should be doubled. . . ." This sale of residential property in Roslyn occurred at about the peak of the city's population, which some estimated to be as high as 4,000 by 1915.

During its heyday, Roslyn served as the commercial center for the two nearby communities of Ronald and Jonesville. Jonesville was a strictly residential town that grew up around the Roslyn Fuel Company's mines about a mile beyond Ronald, reaching a population peak of around 300 persons. Ronald had a post office and some business establishments, including a company store and two taverns. However, many shopping needs of residents of either community could only be met by coming to Roslyn.

Although both towns existed to house coal miners and their families, the communities met completely different fates. Jonesville, which officially was known as Beekman, simply folded up during the mid twenties when the Roslyn Fuel Company closed its mines. Its houses were razed or moved, and it subsequently became an industrial site (currently occupied by the Alpine Veneer Company plant).

The primary reason for Ronald's existence was the N.W.I.'s Number 3 mine. But while the mine ceased production in 1958, the unincorporated community has persisted. During the mid sixties Ronald officially lost its company town status after the Northern Pacific filed a town plat with the county assessor and sold the residential lots to

This photograph shows a portion of Jonesville in 1914.
Photograph courtesy of the Roslyn Museum.

homeowners.

Both the town and its namesake have known moments of colorful history. Decades after the strikebreaking activities of the Northern Pacific and the company's mine manager, Alexander Ronald, had faded from memory, the town became important as a source for alcohol during Prohibition. An enterprising Ronald resident is said to have operated a 250-gallon capacity still in a secret room excavated under Falcon Hall. The still, which was perhaps the largest in the state, escaped detection by revenue agents until a fateful day in 1928 when the apparatus exploded, claiming the life of its operator and starting a fire that consumed more than thirty residences.

These "coal towns" in the Cascades—Roslyn, Ronald, Cle Elum, and for a time Jonesville—shared many common concerns about the quality of daily life and the future of the coal industry. Outside the mines men and their families organized a community life that alternately accentuated or minimized national, linguistic, and socioeconomic differences. For hundreds of men, one social equalizer was work in the mines, which confronted men at every pay level with many common dangers and occupational hazards.

CHAPTER 6

Mining King Coal

The claim has been made that Cle Elum's pioneer founders, Walter Reed and Thomas Gamble, foresaw the emergence at Cle Elum of a "second Pittsburgh."[1] Whether Reed or Gamble held dear such hopes or not we cannot confirm. But the historical record does offer much evidence of ambitious plans for the economic development of the upper county, especially for a decade or more after 1895. In that period the economy of the state of Washington enjoyed an expansionary phase as the nation recovered from the severe financial panic and general business depression of 1893–95.

Coal production figures tell part of the story. Kittitas County output had grown to more than a quarter million tons in the year prior to the panic of 1893. The depression resulted in a momentary slackening of railroad demand for coal, and tonnage dropped for two consecutive years. It recovered somewhat in 1895, but then started a steady climb during the last three years of the century. By 1901 Kittitas County production topped one million tons and then reached near record levels of 1,376,000 tons in 1903.

This sustained climb in production, where each year topped the last, stimulated optimism among coal mine operators and would-be producers. Knowledgeable mining men combed the hills around Roslyn in an attempt to locate coal situated outside the confines of the Northern Pacific land grant. One of the earliest of these men, and the

most prominent, was Archibald S. Patrick, a member of the Northern Pacific's original prospecting crew of 1886.

More than a decade passed between the time that Patrick's employment with the Northern Pacific ended and the establishment of the mining company that later became the Roslyn Cascade Coal Company. Some of these years Patrick spent away from Roslyn, prospecting for coal in northwestern Washington and in British Columbia. Then, as a city employee, Patrick devoted additional time to installing Roslyn's first water system. While in Roslyn, Patrick began—literally—to establish the groundwork for his future mining venture.

At night Patrick stole into the wooded hills above Roslyn to survey section lines and set corner markers, in anticipation of patenting his claim to several sections of land bearing high quality coal in the Roslyn field. According to his grandson, also named Archie S. Patrick, the elder Patrick lost a substantial portion of his claim to the Northern Pacific Railway through subsequent litigation. What remained was a little more than one section of land at the western edge of the Roslyn coal field's most valuable deposits. Development of the property began after Patrick brought in partners. Commercial production of coal began in 1904, one year before Patrick reincorporated the firm as the Roslyn Cascade Coal Company. Of all the independently owned mines in Kittitas County, the Roslyn Cascade Coal Company

A Northern Pacific spur curves gracefully into the city of Roslyn from the N.W.I. Number 8 mine tipple (on facing page).
Photograph courtesy of the Roslyn Museum.

Men and boys alike took their lunch buckets to work in the mines at Cle Elum.
Photograph courtesy of Albert Schober.

proved to be the most enduring and the most successful.

Other independent operators nurtured dreams of similar fortune, but few other operators achieved Patrick's success. The Cle Elum Coal Company began independent production first, when it opened its mine in 1894 on land leased from pioneer resident Thomas L. Gamble. Also producing some coal about this time was the Keelan and Ward mine north of Roslyn. But the most serious competitor to Roslyn Cascade was the Roslyn Fuel Company, which out-produced the Patrick mine after it opened in 1907. Roslyn Fuel accessed the "Roslyn" or five-seam on property that adjoined the Patrick mine north of Ronald. Three years later Roslyn Fuel's second mine gave the company entry into the "big dirty" or one-seam of coal.

For the most part, the other independent mines were small operations that employed only a small number of men besides their owner-operators. As a rule these mines were located on the edge of the Roslyn field, such as the workings near Lakedale, or were sandwiched among the far vaster holdings of the Northwestern Improvement Company along the Roslyn–Cle Elum Ridge on small parcels of land that had escaped consolidation into the Northern Pacific's holdings. Included in some lists of mines are a few workings that remained no more than quickly abandoned prospect tunnels.

The Lakedale operators included Thomas B. Wright, a miner who came to Roslyn in 1887 with three companions from Wilkeson in Pierce County. *Spawn of Coal Dust* tells of a midwinter crossing on foot of the Cascades, and their arrival in a Roslyn of only a few log cabins on New Year's Day of 1887.[2] Wright apparently worked for the N.W.I. at first, for it was not until 1908 that the "Wright Mine" began to produce coal from eight-seam deposits at the southern end of what is now the Pinelochsun residential development. Other Lakedale workings included mining of the seven or "Green" seam, and Amable F. Plant's production from the six-seam.

Further to the east, at Beekman, D. A. Brown opened a small mine into the "big dirty" seam and produced coal for two years. In this same area the Busy Bee Mining and Development Company got a thirty-five-year head start on most other operators by undertaking a small strip mining operation in what is now the backyard of the Alpine Veneer plant. From Ronald eastward to Cle Elum the Northwestern Improvement Company owned almost all of the Roslyn field, with the exception of the small "K & E" mine, later operated by the Yakima Roslyn Coal Company. Finally, at the Cle Elum end of the field, operations independent of the N.W.I. included the Summit mine (later operated by Roslyn Fuel), and the Independent Coal and Coke's Queen mine.

The first decade of recovery from the panic of 1893–95 proved to be the halcyon days for coal mine operators in the state of Washington. Every operator found a market for his coal during this period, and new entrants were encouraged to enter the business. However, low wages also contributed to owner prosperity in these last remaining years before the recognition of the miners' union in Washington.[3]

During the 1890s and the first decade of the twentieth century Washington mine operators had hired increasing numbers of immigrants from southern and central Europe. These men displaced miners of American, English, Scotch, and Welsh nationalities, for the immigrants had lower wage expectations than native workers or longer-established immigrant groups. One consequence was that the labor market continued depressed even after market conditions for coal turned more favorable in the late 1890s. Another consequence was

The N.W.I. Number 9 mine at Roslyn produced coal until 1962.
Photograph courtesy of the Roslyn Museum.

heightened difficulties for union organizers, for the new immigrants had limited English language proficiency and greater fear of jeopardizing their employment.

After the collapse of the Knights of Labor in Washington around 1890, the next major labor union to attempt to organize Washington coal miners was the United Mine Workers of America. Representatives of this union arrived in Washington in 1901 or 1902, and immediately set to work. By 1904 the union claimed to have as many as 3,000 members statewide, with half of these in Roslyn. Faithful to the tradition established by the Northern Pacific, the Northwestern Improvement Company refused to bargain with the union and won the first two strikes that had recognition as their purpose. Shortly afterwards, in 1904, the N.W.I. became the first Washington operator to recognize the United Mine workers of America.

This abrupt change of heart was prompted by the arrival in Washington of organizers from the more radical Western Federation of Miners. By 1903 this group had recruited around four hundred members in Roslyn. The union had a reputation for stirring up labor unrest, a condition that N.W.I. management personnel wished to avoid during boom years for coal. The result was recognition of the U.M.W.A. in Roslyn and the signing of a union contract dated 1 September 1904. The N.W.I. took this step at a time when the Roslyn U.M.W.A. local had lost all but forty-two of its members to the rival W.F.M. But the settlement was the first ever for a Washington coal mine, and set a precedent that other operators soon followed.

The future of the labor movement in Washington coal mines would ultimately follow the fortunes of the Washington coal industry. While the latter prospered, so too did the miners. A temporary slowdown in

coal sales during 1905 and 1906 allowed the U.M.W.A. little room to bargain for contract improvements. But an upswing in the coal market in early 1907 led to the negotiation of a revised contract in February that awarded the union one of its most important demands: the "checkoff" or payroll deduction for union dues. In the meantime, the union had also negotiated an eight-hour day and some wage increases. But unfortunately for miners, further improvement in coal market conditions was not assured.

The first hint that the coal mining industry in the state of Washington faced an uncertain future had surfaced in 1904. In that year coal production declined statewide for the first time since 1893. War in the Pacific between Russia and Japan that disrupted shipping was one reason for lessened demand. But two other reasons portended longer-range problems. In his annual report on coal mines, the state's chief mining inspector alluded to the increasing competitiveness of California fuel oil and to a rapidly increasing use in the Northwest of "electric power produced by our mountain streams." In 1904, only the domestic consumption of coal was "increasing rapidly."[4]

Production of Washington coal decreased for the second straight year in 1905, off two percent from the previous year's figures. The state mining inspector attributed the soft market again to competition from California fuel oil, and to the importation into Washington of cheaper coal from Wyoming and elsewhere.

This two-year decline in coal output ended in 1906. In 1907 production figures set new record levels both for Kittitas County and Washington state. The chief causes for growth in demand was an increasing population and use of domestic and steam coals, and supply shortages of out-of-state coals. Washington mine operators enjoyed the best of times, and the state mining inspector noted with satisfaction that "the coal mining industry seems to be keeping pace with the rapidly growing industries of the state."[5]

Following a single down year in 1908, Washington coal mine operators experienced two more years of increasing output. Statewide coal production in 1910 exceeded 3,979,000 tons, the highest level yet attained and one that was only surpassed during the two war mobilization years of 1917 and 1918. Few observers at the time realized that a turning point in the industry's fortunes had been reached, and that coal mines would soon enter a protracted period of decline.

The state mining inspector found the statistics for 1911 and 1912 to be "not encouraging." During this biennium, most of the gains in output of the previous five years were erased, and in Kittitas county production slumped to the level reached in 1902.

Much of the market lost was due to "the substitution of oil as fuel on a large percentage of steamers running out of Puget Sound ports," and of conversions to oil burning in railroad locomotives and electric generating plants. The state mining inspector, joining dozens of mine owners, wondered "how long will oil sell so cheap?"[6]

If one eliminates from consideration the brief upward blips of the World War I era, the coal industry in Washington began its decline after the peak year of 1910. Closures of the Summit mine in 1909 and the Busy Bee mine in 1911 presaged serious difficulties for small operators and lower profits at the larger operations. Coal, once a primary source of energy for industry, transportation, and domestic heat, began a transition before World War I into the role of a "marginal" fuel supply, one to be tapped when supplies of others ran short.

Wood-sided boxcars and outside-braced coal hoppers await switching in the Northern Pacific yard and coal loading dock at Cle Elum.
Photograph courtesy of Albert Schober.

The marginal status of coal is evident from larger fluctuations in output from 1907 to about 1924. For almost two decades, production fell and then rebounded. The last drop before World War I dealt a severe blow to the industry in 1914 and 1915, as coal output statewide and in Kittitas county fell to turn of the century levels. The state mining inspector attributed the decline to three factors: a mild winter during 1914–15, a general business depression, and increased consumption of fuel oil. The same source reported a year later that the advancing cost of fuel oil had tipped the cost advantage toward coal for railroad use, and that mines were scheduled to reopen. This was the beginning of Washington state's last major surge in coal production—one that resulted in record outputs of 4 million and 4.1 million tons statewide in 1917 and 1918.[7]

Industry observers recognized that Washington coal presented serious competitive disadvantages, however. Coal prices in Washington in 1917 exceeded those in the eastern United States. Numerous reasons for the disparity were cited. Lower per capita output by Washington miners meant higher costs per ton. Other factors included higher

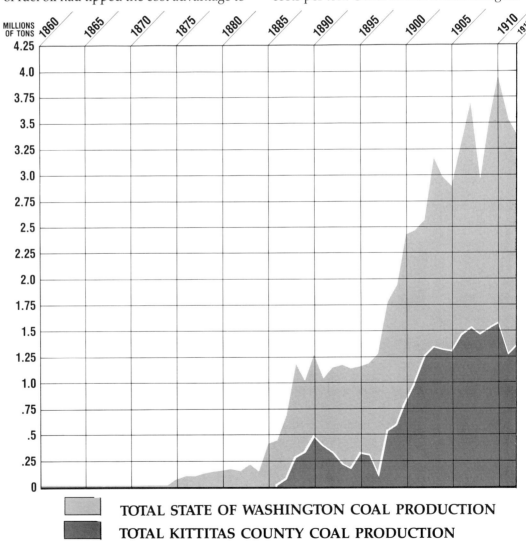

TOTAL STATE OF WASHINGTON COAL PRODUCTION
TOTAL KITTITAS COUNTY COAL PRODUCTION

costs for supplies, numerous folds and faults in the coal fields, difficulties in separating coal from mining waste inside the mine due to steep inclines, and the high cost of transportation.

By 1919 the future of the coal mining industry in Washington appeared "problematical" to the state mining inspector. He cited high costs and competition from electricity, which he noted that the Milwaukee Road was "now using exclusively" on its Seattle to Othello division. One more nail in the coffin of Washington coal was the "marked increase" that year of shipments of lower-

cost coal from Utah and Wyoming.[8]

The all time annual production record for Kittitas county coal was not set until 1920, when county output exceeded 1.8 million tons. Previous record years in 1917 and 1918 had fallen just short of 1.75 million tons. The reason for this record output two years after Washington state had reached its all time peak may be found in increased railroad demand due to a local three-week strike in the N.W.I. mines in Roslyn and Cle Elum in May 1919 and a national strike later that year that closed all the mines in the state.

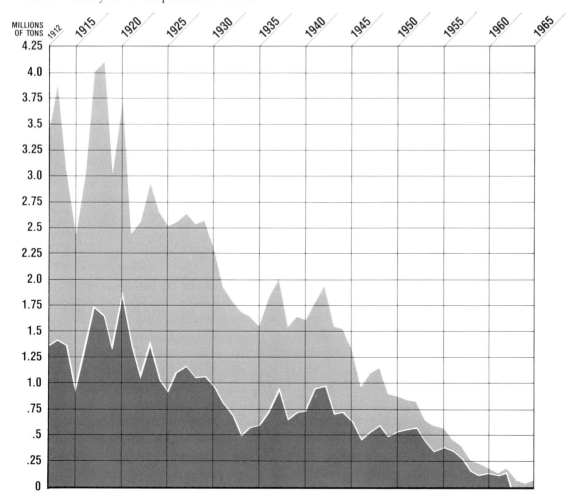

Early Mining Methods

Mining coal in Roslyn's early days was largely a matter of hard manual labor. At the coal face miners used hand picks until the mid 1920s, aided by black powder explosives fired in the coal by the miners themselves or by specialized "shot lighters." The miners worked long "rooms" of coal forty feet wide that often extended hundreds of feet to the boundary of the mine. As the work progressed, timbermen supported the roof with wooden beams held in place by six-inch diameter poles. Between the different mine levels barrier pillars of coal were left to support the limestone roof "cap rock." These barriers were left in place as long as mining extended further into the mine, and then were pulled as the miners retreated back toward the entry.

To transport the coal from the face to the surface, tracklayers installed lightweight 3 or 3½-foot-gauge track in the gangways. Until 1926, mules hauled trips of loaded coal to the surface in some mines, while in other mines electric locomotives or counterbalanced steel cable systems powered by steam provided the lifting power. In addition to tracklayers and mule skinners, coal haulage provided work in the mines to motormen, rope riders, hoist men, and parting boys. Other inside employees included pumpmen, cagers, greasers and trappers. Outside mine workers included men and boys involved in the sorting and loading of coal, as well as those whose occupations like blacksmith, machinist, or carpenter supported the work of men working on the inside.

Early coal mining was hazardous. Annual reports of the Washington state coal mining inspector described with near clinical detail the loss of life and limb from collapsed roof rock, electrocution, falls from moving coal trips, and other assorted causes. Injuries and fatalities most often occurred singly, and, according to the mining inspector, happened mainly because of individual carelessness or disregard for safe mining practices.

At other times, accidents affected the safety of entire crews. For example, every miner shared an interest in assuring adequate mine ventilation. And supervisors and miners alike had to observe rules designed to prevent explosions. Failure to do so led to tragic consequences, like the explosion that rocked N.W.I.'s Number 1 mine in Roslyn on 10 May 1892. The blast killed forty-five miners, left twenty-nine widows, and orphaned ninety-one children.

Clues to the origin of the tragedy were sought during thorough investigations by a committee of miners, a committee of mine managers and superintendents, and the state mining inspector. The evidence was presented to a coronor's jury which ruled that the miners had died from an explosion of gas caused by deficient ventilation. After suits were filed, the Northern Pacific settled most survivors' claims with $1,000 payments to widows or $500 payments to families where a son survived and continued to work in the mines.

The state mining inspector's reports for two decades after the Roslyn disaster of 1892 furnish some explanations for lapses in mine safety. In the 1894 report the inspector complained that miners were obstructing airways with mining debris, and recommended that superintendents discipline the offenders. Two years later the same mining inspector concluded that improper ventilation and other deficiencies in mining technique could be traced to ignorance on the part of mine operators as well.

One year after mining ventilation and inspection requirements became a legislative issue, the mining inspector wrote that "a certain class of political orators and newspapers endeavored to make the miners of this state

The N.W.I. Number 4 mine powerhouse and shaft is pictured above before the explosion.
Photograph courtesy of the Roslyn Museum.

believe that if this bill had become a law mine disasters, such as explosions of fire damp, would not occur. This is an insult to the intelligence of the miners. . . . The first and best thing to do would be to enact a law requiring those in charge of our mines to pass an examination in the theory and practice of mining. This would be the means of raising the standard of efficiency of our mine officials."[9]

Before stepping down as state mining inspector in 1905, C. F. Owen again addressed the question of mine safety in his annual report to the governor. According to Owen, "the high percentage of fatal accidents to the amount of coal mined in this state that has been maintained since the state engaged in the coal mining industry, is due mainly to the reckless and extravagant use of explosives. This is, however, not only true in this state, but is also the fact to a greater or lesser extent in all coal mines in this country wherever powder is used. It is, however, difficult to regulate the proper use of explosives

in the hands of miners. Were a system of more thorough mining and cutting the coal adopted and competent shot lighters employed, the danger in this respect would be reduced."[10]

The question of the competency of miners surfaced in more than one context from the late 1890s to 1910, the industry's period of greatest expansion. During this period the

On 3 October 1909 an explosion rocked the area, and smoke obscured the scene (below).
Photograph courtesy of Albert Schober.

number of miners employed jumped dramatically as Roslyn production rose from an average quarter million tons per year during the mid 1890s to more than 1 million tons in 1901 and more than 1.5 million tons by 1907. Since many lives depended upon strict compliance with safety precautions, any real or supposed shortcomings among miners was a source for alarm.

In his 1907 report, David Botting, the new state coal mining inspector, reported that the industry was making improvements "to enhance the sanitary conditions of the

Fire erupted from the mine shaft (above), leaving an aftermath of destruction (right) and despair (below).
Photograph courtesy of Albert Schober.

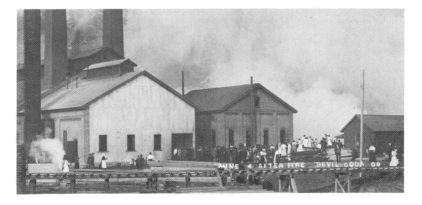

mines and toward safeguarding the lives of employees." But according to Botting, the "unprecedented prosperity in other lines of industry during the first nine months of the year caused the majority of English speaking coal miners to enter into other pursuits, compelling the operators to employ inexperienced foreign immigrants. With this kind of mine labor, the cost of production has materially increased, as has also the liability of damage to life and property."[11]

Mine rescue techniques are demonstrated by a team from the Roslyn Fuel Company.
Photograph courtesy of the Roslyn Museum.

Regardless of the national origins of the miners, hazardous conditions continued to recur inside the mines. On 3 October 1909 a blast rocked the N.W.I. Number 4 mine in Roslyn, claiming ten lives and leaving nine widows and twenty-one orphans. Flames from the explosion "burst out in a pillar 100–400 feet high, and set fire to the head frame, tipple, snowsheds and other nearby buildings."[12]

In 1911 mine safety formed the subject of a special report by Botting and H. M. Wolflin of the U.S. Bureau of Mines. They concluded that the death rate in Washington was "considerably higher" than in the East or central United States, but that the causes were not apparent. "The percentage of English speaking miners and laborers about Washington mines is higher than in many other states," the report stated, "but these men, while more intelligent than the foreigners, are often much more reckless

and take chances they should not take." On balance the report concluded that mining conditions in Washington were more dangerous, especially due to the steep pitch of many coal fields. According to the experts, pitch was a major factor in thirty-six percent of all fatalities during the previous seven years, along with inadequate mine supervision by company officials and miners' recklessness.[13]

The safety report described the norm of mining operations throughout the state, rather than the specific experience at Roslyn and Cle Elum. There is good reason to believe that Kittitas County mines were among the state's safest. First, the pitch of the mines in the Roslyn field, which varied between nine and thirty degrees, was less steep than on the western slope of the Cascades. A second factor was an emphasis on mine safety, exemplified by the quality of the mine rescue teams that were organized in Roslyn and Cle Elum by 1910.

N.W.I. miners from Roslyn and Cle Elum were among the first enrolled at a new mine rescue training center that opened at the University of Washington during 1909. In addition to training, Roslyn mine operators purchased newly developed helmets that improved the potential for success in mine rescue operations. The "Draeger Rescue Apparatus" featured an attached breathing apparatus and oxygen cylinders that allowed entry into mines filled with smoke and poisonous gases. Of a total of thirty-one Draeger helmets in the state in 1910, the N.W.I. at Roslyn had the most with six, while the independent Roslyn Fuel Company owned three. The helmet saw its first use after the fatal 1909 explosion in Roslyn.

In 1912 the state mining inspector credited the N.W.I. for "organizing and training rescue and first aid teams with a greater measure of success than any of the other mining companies." He noted that the N.W.I. sent its Roslyn team to a national mine safety meet in Pittsburgh, Pennsylvania, held on 30–31 October 1911. "This team attracted a great deal of attention, both by the quality of its work and because of its having come the breadth of the continent to be present at the First National Mine Safety Demonstration ever held in America." A year later in Montana the Roslyn team came home with a copper cup and top spot in a first aid contest held at the Montana State Fair.[14]

The first mine rescue and first aid meet in Washington took place in July 1914 and drew eight participants—half from Kittitas County. Three of the entrants were N.W.I. units (two Roslyn, one Cle Elum), plus Roslyn Fuel's team. The Roslyn Fuel team won first place in mine rescue and second place in first aid, while the Cle Elum N.W.I. team earned top honors in first aid. A Roslyn N.W.I. unit finished third in the mine rescue competition.

The Roslyn N.W.I. machine shop stocked horseshoes for mine mules around 1910.
Photograph courtesy of Albert Schober.

The flood of 1908 took a heavy toll on this railroad bridge across the Yakima River.
Photograph courtesy of Albert Schober.

This attention to safety added up to many lives spared. In the period from 1905 to 1916 the best safety record in the state was established by the Roslyn Cascade Coal Company, which mined 615,500 tons of coal without a fatality. At mines where fatalities had occurred, the best production per fatality was registered at Roslyn Fuel's Beekman Number 2 mine, with 450,520 tons mined per fatality. By comparison, the statewide average was one fatality for every 122,000 tons mined.

The communities of Roslyn and Cle Elum lived with the hazards of coal mining for many decades. The work was hard and the potential for grief was immense, even in the best of mines. A fatality for every so many hundred thousand tons of coal mined was still an industrial accident that claimed the life of a father, a husband, or a son. And such statistics do not include those who died slow deaths from the effects of black lung disease.

One man's perspective on the grimness of a coal miner's life saw print on 2 February 1971 when the *Seattle Times* published the thoughts of Ray Rupert, a native of Jonesville. He mused that it was "interesting to read the comments of old-time ex-miners who say they would gladly take up the pick and shovel and ride the mantrip deep into the shafts to mine coal again. Perhaps they remember only the good times. But scattered around the Pacific Northwest are Roslyn coal miners' sons who managed to break free. They remember the good times, too. But they also remember the terrible price which could be exacted deep in the earth."

CHAPTER 7

Logging in Kittitas County

Forests, logging, and the wood products industry have played an important and varied role during the one hundred year history of Cle Elum and Roslyn. Thick forests posed an obstacle to early farmers, ranchers, and townbuilders, and at first far more timber was cut than could ever be used. In a second phase, which began during the time when coal reigned as industrial king and continued for many years after, trees became merchantable, and logging and lumber mills contributed significantly to the Kittitas County economy. Following this period, groups concerned about the environment have adopted protective attitudes toward forest resources. The actions of such individuals have furnished new challenges to the corporations that harvest and process timber products.

In an era that places high value upon the conservation of natural resources, it is difficult to imagine a period when vast stands of pine, hemlock, and fir were felled and summarily burned. Yet, for many nineteenth century Americans the nation's forests were inexhaustible, and merited no better treatment than that given by a gardener to his weeds. As the United States expanded westward, farmers cleared timber from their land following the common sense reasoning that people could eat wheat and corn but not trees.

As America grew, the nation's northern tier yielded up its forests for lumber. First in Maine, then in the states of Michigan,

Wisconsin, and Minnesota, timbermen harvested huge quantities of trees, creating both building materials and tall Paul Bunyan legends in the process. By the end of the century's third quarter, the unimaginable approached reality. Unrestrained first-growth cutting had severely depleted the "inexhaustible" forests. New supplies of virgin timberlands now existed mainly in the Pacific Northwest.

Completion of transcontinental railroads to the Pacific Northwest in the 1880s and 1890s stimulated the growth of a timber industry in Oregon and Washington. The railroads themselves provided a start for many small lumber mills that produced ties for tracklaying, and lumber for water towers, bridges, and other structures. Other mills

Vern St. John and his team pause for this photo in Roslyn in 1912.
Photograph courtesy of the Roslyn Museum.

Cascade Lumber Company loggers work their harvest down the Teanaway River (on facing page).
Photograph courtesy of Jack Whitnall.

A Cascade Lumber Company Shay locomotive awaits loading of flat cars with logs.
Photograph courtesy of Jack Whitnall.

The M. C. Miller Company sawmill and incinerator are pictured in this photograph from 1920.
Photograph courtesy of Albert Schober.

sprang up to meet the needs of small communities such as Cle Elum and Roslyn. In Kittitas County alone, fourteen small mills turned out lumber products, mostly for local consumption.

Two factors brought significant change to the industry around the turn of the century. First, technological advances improved the quality of lumber products, raised millsite capital costs, and put pressure on less efficient, smaller operations. Second, timbermen from the Midwest made major timberland acquisitions in Washington state. In one record-making land transfer in 1900, the Northern Pacific Railway sold 900,000 acres of timberland west of the Cascades to George Weyerhaeuser. This sale catapulted his company to the first rank of Washington timber interests.

In 1902 a different group of midwestern investors founded the Cascade Lumber Company. The firm established its headquarters and mill in Yakima, and began operations with timber purchased in the Teanaway drainage of Kittitas County. The major challenge for Cascade during its early years was transporting logs from the woods to a mill forty to seventy miles away. Cascade first responded with horse logging and river drives, two decidedly low-technology methods that placed a high premium on the strength and skills of in-

dividual timbermen.

Cascade's logging operations in the Teanaway had an immediate impact upon Cle Elum. In 1903 the company opened a store there, both to supply its logging camps and to "pick up such trade as we can in the general store line." This operation initiated the continuous presence in the community of employees of the Cascade Lumber Company and its modern corporate successor, the Boise Cascade Corporation.

During its first thirteen years of operation in the Teanaway, Cascade Lumber conducted annual river drives each spring to

Horse teams provided short-distance motive power in the Teanaway during logging operations.
Photograph courtesy of Albert Schober.

Cascade Lumber Company "bateaus" brought provisions to hungry loggers camped alongside the Yakima River during log drives.
Photograph courtesy of Albert Schober.

Raging waters sometimes dumped logs outside the river's main channel. Loggers had to prod them back in.
Photograph courtesy of Albert Schober.

transport logs that had wintered over. The drives provided daily tests of skill and endurance for loggers who often spent whole days, from sunrise to sunset, in the ice cold river waters. The log drives consumed five or six weeks, and provided something like a traveling road show for the communities situated along the banks of the Yakima River. Children and adults alike flocked to watch the nimble-footed prowess of rugged men as they pried, coaxed, and manhandled logs. Corralling and refloating strays and dynamiting jams furnished constant challenges as the drive progressed at an

average rate of two to three miles per day.

Following the log drives, the Cascade loggers spent another six months in the woods cutting trees. The work employed fellers (the logging elite) and buckers (men who cut logs in lengths). But it also required road-builders, teamsters, swampers (men who cleared the ground for the horses), and last but not least, camp cooks. The latter cooked four meals a day to fuel mighty men who chopped and sawed first-growth trees as large as five feet in diameter that towered upward two hundred feet or more.

During the early years of Cascade's opera-

This group of loggers relax after an outdoor meal near Cle Elum.
Photograph courtesy of Albert Schober.

tions in the Teanaway, the company's crew of loggers attracted Slavs, Italians, Finns, Swedes, and Greeks. Many were "floaters"—men who drifted from camp to camp—who wintered in Seattle and returned penniless each spring to start a new year. They were steeped in logging traditions and observed a common etiquette. This included such practices as cookhouse meals consumed in silence, shared songs for work and relaxation, and a commonly understood division of labor.

Northwest lumbermen, like their eastern and midwestern predecessors, had learned to live a rugged outdoors life in the woods. As long as the camp food was both good and plentiful, most loggers stoically accepted hard working conditions. But there were limits. During the teens many North-

west loggers joined or sympathized with the Industrial Workers of the World, a radical labor union that reached a peak of strength in the years leading up to the entry of the United States into World War I.

In 1917 the I.W.W. organized a strike honored by nearly all Northwest loggers. In addition to higher pay, the union demanded improved working conditions. Among these was the eight-hour day, which by this time had already become a standard throughout most of the United States, and company furnished bunkhouse sheets and blankets. The latter issue assumed great symbolic importance for the union, especially after the I.W.W. called for its members to "burn their bindles" in a mass demonstration of defiance. The bindles were bedrolls that loggers carried with them from camp to camp,

Railroad logging mechanized only a portion of the hard work of harvesting trees in the Teanway.
Photograph courtesy of Jack Whitnall.

Cascade Lumber Company bunk cars gave shelter to hardy loggers.
Photograph courtesy of Jack Whitnall.

in an attempt to secure some level of warmth and comfort. Despite concerted employer opposition, Northwest loggers won this battle, though the I.W.W. soon disintegrated in an increasingly hostile environment for leftist union movements.

The new working conditions of the late teens were accompanied in Kittitas County by a change in operations by Cascade Lumber Company. In 1913 the firm concluded that its river drive method of transporting logs to the mill in Yakima was a money-losing proposition. The river drives had some limitations that the company could simply not control. Every year, for instance, rapid spring runoff water carried logs down overflowing river banks and beached many on the adjacent lands of Kittitas County farmers. Not a year passed that Cascade did not adjudicate or settle lawsuits

brought by landowners for damage to their crops, livestock, or structures.

Another problem was losing logs that either could not be retrieved, or that escaped the holding ponds near the Yakima mill and sped merrily on toward Portland and an ocean rendezvous. Water that raged could also be still, and this occasioned additional difficulties during those years when a low river volume limited the number of logs that the Yakima could carry to the mill. Finally, the procedure was lengthy and costly in terms of manpower.

For all these reasons, the Cascade Lumber Company decided to abandon river drives in favor of railroad logging. It also decided in 1913 to replace timber buying in the Teanaway with land purchases, and soon acquired title to half of the land in the drainage. Fortunately for Cascade, the last river

This contraption that looks like an overgrown snowmobile pulled logs during the winter.
Photograph courtesy of Jack Whitnall.

drive occurred in the spring of 1916, just one season before the big floods of the spring of 1917. This timing was most fortunate, for had the company stacked logs on the rivers during the previous fall and winter, the extreme runoff conditions in 1917 would surely have caused rampaging logs to demolish most bridges in their path.

As it was, the raging waters washed out much of the track that Cascade had laid to its new operational headquarters at Casland. Casland—a name coined by combining "Cascade" and "land"—was built at

the junction of the middle and the west forks of the Teanaway River, and served as the point of departure for shipping logs to Yakima for the next thirteen years.

Feeding logs to Casland was the task of the loggers who worked in numerous backwoods camps. Families were housed in portable wooden homes mounted on stilts that were moved from one location to another on railroad flat cars. Single men, on the other hand, shared small bunk cars parked on a siding. Other temporary structures, such as barns for the dozen or more work horses and the mess house, completed the camp.

At first, Cascade's railroad logging operation mechanized no more than the final transportation of logs from the backwoods camp to the mill. Horses were still used to skid logs from the mountain side to the temporary spurs built by tracklayers up the many creeks that are tributary to the Teanaway River. Once loaded, a Shay geared locomotive hauled the day's cut of logs back to Casland. There a larger branch line locomotive took over, depositing the loaded cars at the Northern Pacific siding at Teanaway for transshipment to Yakima.

During the 1920s, however, increased mechanization transformed work in the logging camps. The chain saw, an implement that one old-time logger remarked could do the work of twenty-five men, made its appearance during this decade along with Caterpillar tractors. For Paul Lee, who once worked in the Teanaway, automation doomed to extinction a life style that had much intrinsic merit. The chain saw in particular, Lee said, caused "the ruination of the country."[1]

Another observer, Jack Whitnall of Yakima, has reached a different conclusion. Whitnall, a second-generation commercial photographer whose father preceded him as photographer for Cascade Lumber, wrote that "the first fifty years of Cascade's logging on the Yakima River used practically every method and tool devised since the New England lumber boom of the two centuries ago. The 'weak mind, strong back' era has become the age of levers and pushbuttons directing amazing machines. Each step of this evolutionary process has made for less danger to men, and less cost of logs in the pond. Each step has made for better forestry, more timber crop per year, and better utilization of the log in the mill."[2]

The ultimate automation of Pacific North-

west logging still remained to come when Cascade Lumber closed its Casland operation in 1930. Although lumber prices and volumes declined during the Depression, Cascade continued railroad logging in the nearby Swauk Creek area until finally abandoning the method in 1944. For nearly thirty years, railroad logging allowed Cascade Lumber to overcome the disadvantage of producing logs for a distant mill. In the postwar period, the even more flexible truck transportation system reduced log delivery times even further, and introduced greater economies. By this time, however, the turn-of-the-century logging camp was a thing of the past.

CHAPTER 8

Coal's Struggle for Survival

Snow is piled high along First Street in Cle Elum in 1916.
Photograph courtesy of Albert Schober.

For the coal mining industry in Washington state, the four-year period from 1916 to 1920 appeared to justify the optimism that miners and mine operators alike had placed in coal development. Mobilization for World War I sent the economy into high gear for several years, and pushed Washington coal production to record levels. Statewide, an all-time high of 4.1 million tons was reached in 1918, with Kittitas County accounting for 1.7 million tons of that total. Two years later Kittitas County producers topped 1.8 million tons of coal for the only time in the history of the field.

To meet the war demand, miners in Washington state worked more days per year than at any time since the turn of the century. Mine operators paid record wages during this period when all mines in the state operated under union contracts. But in this economy mobilized for war high rates of inflation prevailed. As a result miners sought and received compensatory wage adjustments from federal government administrators that increased miners' pay twice during 1917—first by fourteen percent, then again by fifteen percent.

The demand for coal was so great that operators opened new mines during this period and reactivated older properties that had fallen victim to hard times only a few years before. Unfortunately for both

For residents in 1913, this was "the big snow." On the back of this picture postcard (on facing page), a writer describes the thoroughfare as "Graveyard Street."
Photograph courtesy of Albert Schober.

operators and miners, this demand for fuel was only as temporary as the mobilization for war. The bubble burst as early as 1919, as coal consumption dropped and the economy struggled to absorb soldiers returning home from military service.

The decade that followed the end of World War I affected various sectors of the American economy in different ways. Farm commodity prices dropped steadily, for example, and bankrupted many marginal producers. The transportation industry became intensely competitive, as railroads struggled to compete both against new forms of motor transportation and cheaper coast-to-coast ocean shipping rates made possible by the construction of the Panama Canal. In time, the effects of a budding aviation industry would also diminish the railroads' share of

the total transportation market. On the positive side, industrial output, which lagged briefly during the transition from a wartime to a peacetime economy, increased generally during the twenties, and demand for lumber products kept the Northwest's forests buzzing with activity.

The organization of American workers into labor unions had reached a peak during the war mobilization years. After the war, labor leaders and the rank and file membership alike aspired to consolidate the gains in wages, hours, and working conditions that had been achieved through a struggle of more than two decades, and even to improve upon them. But the desires of labor met stiff resistance from employers, and in 1919 alone nearly four thousand strikes idled one fifth of American labor force. Unfortunately for organized labor, this show of solidarity resulted in more disappointments than gains, as deflation in the immediate postwar years exerted a downward pressure on wages. In Washington state as elsewhere, the labor movement lost momentum after the war. And for Washington coal miners, the labor battles of the early twenties were nothing short of disastrous.

Wage conditions for coal miners nationally had improved significantly since the 1890s when miners worked long days for two and a half dollars. By the end of World War I, union organized miners had won pay raises that brought the earnings of miners to $5.89

World War I recruits prepare to depart Cle Elum.
Photograph courtesy of Albert Schober.

The snowsheds to the Number 1 mine in Roslyn served their function well in 1916.
Photograph courtesy of Albert Schober.

*Loaded coal cars await
movement at the tipple of
the N.W.I. Number 3
mine in Ronald in 1929.*
Photograph courtesy of the
Washington State Historical
Society. Photo by Asahel Curtis.

*In 1935 a smaller facility
in Roslyn replaced this
N.W.I. miners' wash
house and company
stables.*
Photograph courtesy of the
Roslyn Museum.

per eight-hour day. Rapid inflation during the war ate away at those gains, however, and as 1919 began coal miners nationwide chafed to be done with government control of the industry.

In this postwar period social and labor unrest erupted worldwide. In Russia the Red Army, sustained primarily by working class people, ultimately defeated the White Russian coalition of anti-Bolshevik forces in a three-year-long civil war that ended in 1921. A workers' revolution in Hungary in 1919 was less successful, lasting only six months before Romanian troops occupied the capital and brought down the new government. In Germany, however, organized union opposition and an effective general strike, supported by all classes of workers, both white collar and blue, cut short an attempted right-wing coup against a coalition centrist–social democrat government.

This banner of the Cle Elum Local 2512 of the U.M.W.A. hangs in the Roslyn Museum.
Photo by the author.

Closer to home, workers in Seattle organized the nation's first general strike in this turbulent era to protest government intervention in a shipyard strike. The general walkout was called after a telegram from the director of the wartime "Emergency Fleet Corporation" was mistakenly delivered to the Central Labor Council instead of to the shipyard management association. In his message, the director urged management to make no concessions and not to negotiate with labor during the strike. In sympathy, workers belonging to 110 locals voted to participate in a general strike. For five days, 100,000 workers stayed away from their jobs. During this time a strike committee organized workers to maintain essential services, such as laundry for hospitals, and to provide milk at neighborhood distribution points. An unarmed workers' security patrol was provided, but had little to do, for during the strike the crime rate actually dropped in Seattle.

A poem written by a person identified only as Anise and published in the Seattle *Union Record* explained the source of fright among the city's conservatives:
"What scares them most is
That NOTHING HAPPENS!
They are ready
For DISTURBANCES.
They have machine guns
And soldiers,
But this SMILING SILENCE
   Is uncanny.
The businessmen
Don't understand
That sort of weapon. . .
It is your SMILE
That is UPSETTING
Their reliance
   On Artillery, brother!
It is the garbage wagons
That go along the street
Marked 'EXEMPT

by STRIKE COMMITTEE.'
It is the milk stations
That are getting better daily,
And the three hundred
WAR Veterans of Labor
Handling the crowds
WITHOUT GUNS,
For these things speak
Of a NEW POWER
And a NEW WORLD
That they do not feel
At HOME in."[1]

The strike ended just as peaceably as it began, despite the presence nearby of federal troops and a 2,400-member militia hastily deputized by the mayor of Seattle. Some people, including the mayor of Seattle, believed that labor was attempting to mount a revolution against the government and established order. Instead the strike demonstrated a broadly based sympathy for industrial democracy.

Mine workers across America saw a golden opportunity during 1919 to consolidate the gains made in preceding years. Nationally the labor movement was at a peak of strength, and with Europe prostrate, miners believed that fewer immigrants would flow into the United States to offer mine owners a cheap labor alternative. The events in Seattle early in the year reinforced the opinions of U.M.W.A. members that the public "was aroused to a new interest in its laboring members as a part of the democracy which everyone had been straining every nerve to preserve."[2]

Although the coal industry in September 1919 still remained under government control, John L. Lewis, head of the international union in Indianapolis, asked mine operators

John L. Lewis, who led the United Mine Workers of America for decades, is pictured here in 1955.
Photograph courtesy of the Roslyn Museum.

A loading boom deposits coal in the tipple of the N.W.I. Number 3 mine at Ronald.
Photograph courtesy of the Washington State Historical Society. Photo by Asahel Curtis.

to make substantial improvements to existing contracts. Miners wanted a sixty percent wage increase, a six-hour "bank to bank" day (meaning the workday began and ended at the mineworks rather than at the coal face), and a five-day workweek. The operators had made record profits during the war, but refused these demands on grounds of "unreasonableness" and because existing contracts did not begin to expire until April 1920.

The refusal to negotiate prompted the union to call a nationwide coal strike for 1 November 1919. Mine operators remained intransigent, and late in October President Wilson declared the strike illegal and offered to establish a fact finding commission as an alternative to the work stoppage. The miners struck anyway, and within days much of the nation's wheels of industry and transportation began grinding to a halt.

For thirty-six days the country remained paralyzed by the miners' strike, until finally in early December, with coal stocks nearly gone, President Wilson asked the miners to return to work with a fourteen percent wage increase. On a nationwide basis, the strike posed a real threat of economic disruption if it should continue throughout the cold winter months. Thus the government felt justified in imposing a settlement that bound both the mineworkers' union and the mine operators.

Most miners obeyed the back to work order, although a few mine operators refused to accept the terms of the president's decree. Alone in Washington state, the management of the Wilkeson mine in western

Washington began to lock out union miners and to hire nonunion replacements. Such antilabor behavior embittered the miners, and almost caused a further walkout at all Washington mines.

There is no question that Washington coal miners did not want a return to the "bad old days" of before, and that they believed that through union solidarity their demands for improvements in wages and working conditions would be met. The country needed coal, nearly as much as miners could produce, and miners sensed that the bargaining advantage had finally tilted to their side.

The miners' attitude is reflected in the three-week strike of the N.W.I. mines in Roslyn and Cle Elum in May 1919. The union locals called out their men after miners objected to moving coal cars in the mines by pushing them by hand. The mood among miners in Roslyn and Cle Elum was probably little improved by President Wilson's imposed settlement of the six-week-long national strike later in 1919, for work

did not resume in Kittitas County mines until 23 December, a full eight days after miners returned to their jobs in other parts of Washington.

From the miners' point of view, the year 1920 probably brought the highest compensation and the best working conditions compared to any other prior period. The fourteen percent increase awarded by the government in December 1919 raised miners' wages to $6.75 per eight-hour day. Improvements did not stop there, as national negotiations during the spring and summer of 1920 resulted in new contracts in September that raised wages another twenty-two percent, to $8.25 per day.

Trouble was brewing for Washington miners, however. Already the operators were complaining that the fourteen percent increase granted by President Wilson threatened the economic viability of their mines. The result was an increased participation of mine operators in a movement by Washington businessmen to institute the

The deep snow of 1916 was most easily negotiated by teamsters with "four-hooved" drive.
Photograph courtesy of Albert Schober.

Roslyn brewery workers who posed for this picture in 1909 included boys and men.
Photograph courtesy of the Roslyn Museum.

"open shop." This system allowed nonunion workers to compete for jobs by agreeing to work for less than union scale. A second consequence of the operators' concern for profits was the establishment of a commission to study the specific economics of coal mining in Washington.

The commission was a special study group of the United States Bituminous Coal Commission, appointed after the 1919 strike to study labor-management relations. The committee was formed in the spring of 1920 when it became apparent that Washington coal mine conditions varied substantially from those in the "Central Competitive Field." Members included two Washington state union officials, two members of the operators' association, and a Pennsylvania mining engineer named Allport.

The group found that Washington mines indeed presented special problems, and

recommended that a new wage scale add just four cents a day to the rate that miners received after their fourteen percent increase in 1919. The commission's report noted that at this level of wages Washington mines could be operated profitably, but only if production and sales both remained high. The operators accepted the agreement, and a contract was signed that ran from 1 August 1920 to 31 March 1922.

A short time later the United Mineworkers negotiated a raise in wages in the Central Competitive Field to $8.25 per day, a full $1.50 above the top of the scale recommended for Washington miners by the special study group. This proved to be a severe blow to Washington operators who found themselves obliged, in accord with past practice, to adjust their union scales to national standards.

The sale of Washington coal declined dur-

Loaded trips pause at the third-east parting in the N.W.I.'s Number 8 mine in Roslyn.
Photograph courtesy of the Roslyn Museum.

ing the second half of 1920, and continued slow during the winter of 1920–21. The operators claimed that they were losing money on every ton of coal they sold, and pressed for corrective action. Finally, on 28 February 1921, mine operators asked the United Mineworkers in Washington state's District 10 to accept a wage rollback to 1919 levels. The union refused, citing a contract that still had more than a year to run. As a consequence, Washington mine operators closed seventeen mines on 15 March, leaving open only those that provided coal for railroad use, principally the N.W.I. mines of Roslyn and Cle Elum.

Although the N.W.I. miners at Roslyn and Cle Elum were not immediately affected by mine closures, they were to play an important role in the future evolution of one of the state of Washington's most significant labor disputes. While they continued to earn record wages, their fellow union members in western Washington faced an uncertain future.

Within a month after the mine closures, Washington's state government persuaded both sides of the dispute to form a new commission to study the problems and issue a set of recommendations. The members were the same as the year before when the study group acted under the auspices of the United States Bituminous Coal Commission. This "Allport Commission," named after the neutral member from Pennsylvania, convened in late May 1921 and issued its report five weeks later.

The commission recommended wage reductions of from twenty-five to twenty-eight percent, a more economical system of supervision by the operators, and a reduced margin of profit for retail distributors. The commission hoped thereby to recover lost markets by making coal available more economically to the consumer. The key to this plan was reduction of labor costs, with the major saving coming from a rollback of

The Cle Elum High School basketball squad poses for a photograph in 1917.
Photograph courtesy of Albert Schober.

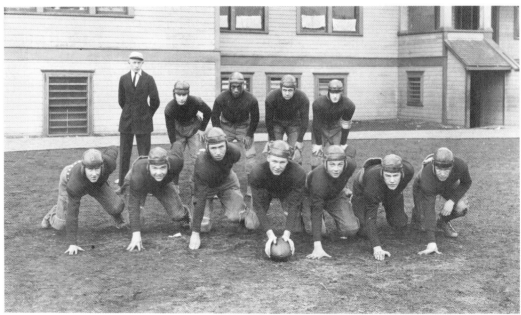

Some mean-looking faces give the 1923 Roslyn High School football team an aggressive appearance.
Photograph courtesy of Albert Schober.

miners' wages to $6.00 per day.

The response of the labor members of this commission was surprisingly moderate. In public comment they noted that "our in-vestigation has revealed a condition of affairs that we are frank to state is more discourag-ing than we had anticipated." They pleaded lack of authority to offer a solution to the problems, and preferred not to recommend a wage rollback that would conflict with established union policy. According to them, such a rollback could only happen with the concurrence of the union's international office and after approval by the union's district membership through a referendum.[3]

Following procedures approved at a special district convention in May, the mineworkers' union prepared in July to poll its members about the Allport Commission recommendations. Ballots were sent to all union locals, including those in Roslyn and Cle Elum where most miners remained on the job. The operators openly criticized the union for polling working miners, and accused its leadership of attempting to engineer the referendum's defeat.

Later events would seem to justify the operators' opinion, although it may be argued that the responsibility for scuttling the rollback proposal lay more with union members at the local level than with District 10 officials. As could be expected, opposition to the plan was most vociferous in Roslyn and Cle Elum. Not content to express their disapproval with ballots, miners from the Roslyn and Cle Elum locals sent telegrams to John L. Lewis at international headquarters, asking whether he had sanctioned the referendum. When the reply came back that he had not, Kittitas County miners protested in mass meetings and ultimately forced district leaders to call off the vote.[4]

The Washington district of the United Mineworkers of America was reaching what one historian of the labor dispute has called "the most critical period in its history."[5] At stake was the principal of labor solidarity and the future of organized labor in the coal mining industry in Washington, as well, perhaps, as the future of the industry itself.

One could hardly expect John L. Lewis,

The Yakima River winds gracefully past Cle Elum—illuminated in a late afternoon, midwinter light.
Photograph courtesy of Albert Schober.

Empty mine trips await another day's service after unloading at the N.W.I. Number 7 mine tipple at Cle Elum.
Photograph courtesy of the Roslyn Museum.

who only two years before had called for a sixty percent wage increase and a thirty-hour workweek, to appear to favor wage reductions for union members in Roslyn and Cle Elum. Nor should one fault the miners in Roslyn and Cle Elum for not anticipating the consequences of refusing to grant concessions to the operators. It is fair to say, however, that union members in Roslyn and Cle Elum, by thwarting the referendum approved by District 10 leadership, denied the rest of the union membership an opportunity to influence its future.

The consequences for union members on the west side of the Cascades were horrendous. Once the mine operators realized that there would be no referendum, they initiated plans to break the union altogether. Ground leases in company towns were terminated, and by September mine operators began to evict striking workers from their homes. Public opinion, which heretofore

had supported the miners, started to favor the operators.

The conflict between union and operators soon assumed statewide significance as Associated Industries, an employer group, attempted to extend the "open shop" movement to the coal industry. Buoyed by the defeat of a strike by Pacific coast International Seamen and Seattle longshoremen, the group encouraged miners to break with the union and return to work. The operators willingly hired them as nonunion labor, but only after a thorough investigation of their work records indicated that they were passive workers and not "trouble makers."[6]

The strike ground on through the autumn of 1921, with union members and their families housed in tent camps provided by the mineworkers' union. The workers were supported by small relief allowances, financed in part by a ten percent assessment on the wages of mineworkers who were still working (mainly in Roslyn and Cle Elum), and by some funds from international headquarters. The strike was also supported by other unions in the Seattle and Tacoma areas, some of which demonstrated their solidarity by sending food and clothing to the tent camps in automobile caravans.

One of the few bright spots in this troubled picture for miners came in October 1921 when the Roslyn Fuel Company and Cle Elum's Independent Coal and Coke Company broke the operators united front and agreed to settle on union terms. It was a rare victory, and, as it happened, provided only a momentary return of labor peace. The mineworkers' contract was coming to an end nationally on 31 March 1922, and the union, under John L. Lewis's leadership, continued to press for a shorter workday. The leadership of District 10 had no choice but to participate in a nationwide strike that shut down all mines for several months beginning 1 April 1922.

The refusal of mine operator associations throughout the country to negotiate with the international union weakened the

mineworkers' organization, and led by summer to a decision to permit local negotiations on a district by district basis. In Washington terms were reached that ended the strike in August 1922. This settlement mainly affected Kittitas County operators, for by this time most of the mine operators in western Washington were committed to the open shop system. Many of these operators must

Advertising before Labor Day in 1921 gives some indication of the popularity of organized labor.
Photograph courtesy of the Roslyn Museum.

John Morusick sprinkled Cle Elum streets with this 1917, solid-tired Maxwell truck that carried 500 gallons of water in its tank.
Photograph courtesy of Albert Schober.

have adopted a pessimistic view about the future of coal mining in Washington, for much of the coal they recovered was in safety pillars and other readily accessible areas that ensured low costs for a few years but also condemned the mines to closure.

The new union contract that went into effect in August 1922 rolled back miners' wages from $8.25 per day to $7.50 per day, with no reduction in hours. In the meantime, the strike continued in western Washington, with operators employing nonunion labor. By this time the conflict had become hopeless for the miners, but the union continued its action until May 1923 when District 10 officials terminated the strike. Union members were authorized to accept work according to the conditions offered by the operators.

Union Politics and the 1934 Strike

The politics of organized labor had an enormous effect upon the social fabric of Roslyn, Ronald, and Cle Elum during the towns' first half century of existence. From the early battles of the Knights of Labor in 1888 to the struggle for recognition by the Western Miners of America in the 1930s, the complex arena of labor relations provided a stage for social interaction. During this period labor politics not only affected residents of Roslyn and Cle Elum as individuals, but also helped to shape the course of organized labor throughout the state.

Recognition by employers of the U.M.W.A. in 1904 and 1905 had resulted in the withdrawal of a competing organization, but did not bring unanimity of opinion to

Northern Pacific coal cars on two tracks are loaded with coal at the N.W.I. Number 7 mine tipple at Cle Elum.

Photograph courtesy of the Washington State Historical Society. Photo by Asahel Curtis.

One of Cle Elum's first taxis was this Overland car operated by Clarence Bostock.
Photograph courtesy of Albert Schober.

Coal glistens on the left side of an undusted portion of the N.W.I. Number 3 mine in Ronald.
Photograph courtesy of the Washington State Historical Society. Photo by Asahel Curtis.

Mine workers keep up a rapid pace at their shaking screen and picking table.

Photograph courtesy of the Washington State Historical Society. Photo by Asahel Curtis.

the labor movement in Kittitas County or to the state as a whole. Within five years, philosophical differences that once separated rival unions emerged within the ranks of the U.M.W.A. membership. As it happened, Roslyn and Cle Elum union locals played an important role in a statewide contest for leadership of District 10. The opponents were John Wallace, a conservative candidate favored by most of the locals in western Washington, and Robert Harlan, a radical whose largest base of support was Kittitas County. In 1910 the two ran against each other for district president, but with inconclusive results. Accusations of ballot fraud caused a split in the organization for nearly two years, until Wallace resigned his post to take a new state position administering a workman's compensation

law that passed the legislature in 1911.

Harlan retained the presidency of the union during the next decade, until a recall campaign that originated in Kittitas County forced him out of office in 1922. By this time he had lost his sheen as a "radical" in the eyes of Kittitas County miners. The latter accused him of selling out to the employer groups when he agreed to put a wage rollback measure to the vote of union members during the early 1920s.

The labor war that pitted miners against coal operators in the early 1920s had left the statewide organization of miners in shambles. Union members in western Washington were forced to choose between unemployment and low paying jobs at open shop mines. And even the jobs that mine operators offered were diminished in number, due to a decline in demand for coal for both industrial and domestic uses.

The defeat of organized labor in Washington's coal mines was only partial, for union contracts remained in force in Kittitas County mines. But the 1920s were bleak years for the industry, especially in Washington, where energy consumers increasingly converted to electricity and petroleum products. Coal mining employment began a steady decline due both to lessened product demand and to the introduction of mechanical mining devices during the mid 1920s.

The unfavorable market for coal during the 1920s resulted in miners working fewer days per year at some mines, or losing their jobs altogether as owners permanently closed down unprofitable operations. After the Independent Coal and Coke Company in Cle Elum and the Roslyn Fuel Company closed their mines in 1927, only two operators of significance remained in Kittitas County—the railroad's Northwestern Improvement Company and the much smaller Roslyn Cascade Coal Company.

Although miners in Kittitas County worked under a union contract and were relatively better off than their counterparts in western Washington, miners' dissatisfaction in Roslyn and Cle Elum began to increase during the late twenties and early thirties. One major issue was the use of automated equipment which had helped raise productivity from 3.5 tons per shift in 1927 to 4.17 tons in 1930. There was a human toll that these figures did not address, however, such as reduced employment in the

A mining machine is photographed in 1929 as it undercuts the coal seam in the N.W.I. Number 3 mine in Ronald.

Photograph courtesy of the Washington State Historical Society. Photo by Asahel Curtis.

mines and increased work for those who remained.

The beginning of the Great Depression accelerated the decline of the Washington coal industry, as the wheels of industry and transport lay idle or turned at a much diminished rate. In Kittitas County, coal production dropped by more than half from a late 1920s peak of 1,198,000 tons in 1927 to 499,000 tons in 1933. As a result, miners' discontent grew and was directed increasingly at John L. Lewis as the national leader of the U.M.W.A.

The ineffectiveness of the U.M.W.A. during the early 1920s to preserve the gains of organized labor and the distance from the union's headquarters in the Midwest contributed to a sense of alienation among many Washington miners. Furthermore, some Washington union members believed that John L. Lewis had helped destroy the coal strike during the 1920s, ostensibly because he resented their opposition to his bid to gain the presidency of the American Federation of Labor.[7]

Such feelings gave added impetus to miners already disgruntled over worsening

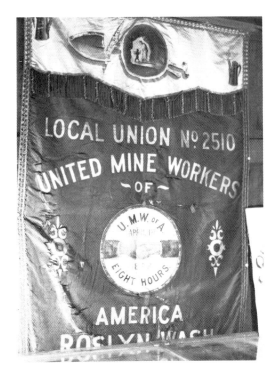

The banner of Roslyn Local 2510 of the United Mine Workers of now adorns the Roslyn Museum.
Photo by the author.

Successful hunters display their deer.
Photograph courtesy of the Roslyn Museum.

wage and labor conditions in Washington mines. In significant numbers, N.W.I. coal miners abandoned the U.M.W.A. for the newly formed Western Miners of America. In the spring of 1934, this organization demanded a new labor election. Rebuffed, the W.M.A. launched a bitter strike that split labor ranks and drew state and national attention to Roslyn.

The prospect for peaceful resolution of the conflict diminished early in the W.M.A.'s campaign when an N.W.I. machinist named Bob Ruff died from a pistol shot in the back as he stood in a group on a Roslyn street. According to local witnesses, his attacker was Sam Farrimond, a U.M.W.A. partisan. Minutes before the crime, Farrimond had announced while drinking in a bar that he was going to kill someone, "to scare the others [Western Miners]." At a subsequent trial, Farrimond was represented by E. K. Brown. According to Clyde Fischer, then a Roslyn justice of the peace, Brown was "a good lawyer, crookeder than hell. If you had the money, he would get you free."[8] After this incident, tension escalated in Roslyn and relations between the two factions, already strained, deteriorated further. Farrimond, in the meantime, was acquitted of the crime.

The conflict intensified in March 1934. A letter published on 2 March in the Cle Elum *Miner-Echo* represented in this way the views of the UMWA: "There are today sinister influences at work within this section which are not for your best interests and we are satisfied that all the well meaning citizens are opposed to."

The following week, on 9 March, the *Miner-Echo* published the W.M.A.'s reply: "In past years the officials of the U.M.W.A. forced upon its membership reductions in wages and the breaking down of working conditions by the dictatorship of John L. Lewis. . . . The U.M.W.A. with the support of company [N.W.I.] officials have used threats and coercion and intimidation against the members of the W.M.A. trying

to force them back to the U.M.W.A."[9]

The W.M.A. decided to strike and on 1 April 1934 pickets went up. A large majority of miners in Roslyn sided with the new union, while only ninety to one hundred miners remained loyal to the U.M.W.A. A week after the strike began, twelve hundred W.M.A. miners, wives, and children marched in support of the union's demand for new elections. But despite this overwhelming expression of support—or perhaps because of it—the U.M.W.A. and the company, with the assistance of the municipal authorities in Roslyn and Cle Elum, worked to suppress the new movement.

An appeal to Washington, D.C., by the mayors of Cle Elum and Roslyn prompted President Roosevelt to send as arbitrator the chairman of the Denver division of the Coal Labor Board. After investigation, he found that the U.M.W.A. contract was valid, since the miners who now belonged to the W.M.A. had worked since 26 October 1933 under its terms and had accepted its

Chief Lloyd Bunker (second from left) of the Cle Elum Police Department poses with his supercharged Graham police car.
Photograph courtesy of Albert Schober.

"A Little Nest of Fascists"

Reprinted from *The New Republic,* 30 May 1934.

Roslyn, in the state of Washington, lies in the mountains about a hundred miles from Seattle, three miles off the Spokane road where it passes through Cle-Elum, with which it is connected by a single strip of pavement. Seen on the map it resembles a toy balloon on a string; cut the string (or throw a force of police across the road) and the balloon is isolated.

Readers of The New Republic who have been following events in Imperial Valley may find some interest in the following recital of the experience of an Englishman and his wife in this other disturbed corner of the West Coast. The experiences were comparatively trivial, but illuminating to the writer (who is a member of the Economics faculty at Oxford and will be hereinafter referred to as the O.U.P., or Oxford University Professor).

Roslyn is the center of a decaying mining area and for some weeks there has been strife between a newly formed local of the United Mine Workers and the Western Miners' Union for the right to represent the workers. Mediators appointed by the federal government found for the United Mine Workers—on what basis the O.U.P. has so far been unable to discover—but the Western Miners' Union declined to accept the decision and remained on strike. The situation became increasingly violent and local papers gave reports of police activities in the area, particularly the breaking of picket lines with tear-gas bombs. It should be mentioned that Roslyn belongs to the Northern Pacific Railway, though apparently the miners in large measure own their homes. All things considered it seemed a good place for the O.U.P. to observe an industrial conflict at first hand. He therefore motored over, accompanied by the district secretary of the I.L.D., Revels Cayton, a young Negro, who was to introduce him to the strikers' committee.

Roslyn, when reached, looked very drear; the houses were faintly reminiscent of those of Southern share-croppers; the streets gave no signs of activity and the general feeling of a state of siege was noticeable. After a brief lunch we drove to the Western Miners' hall, which was locked. Our efforts were observed by members of the state patrol, who promptly closed in. After failing to find that our automobile papers were out of order they invited us to come to headquarters at Cle-Elum for further investigation. There one look at Cayton was enough for the lieutenant. "You're the man who made speeches at Anacortes. You're arrested." Mrs. O.U.P., herself a graduate of law, was a bit surprised at such summary methods and asked if some warrant or legal justification was not necessary. "Oh, no, that's not necessary. He's arrested." "But has he a criminal record?" "No, but we know about him." So exit Cayton.

This was about 1:50 P. M., less than an hour after our arrival. At 2:30 P. M. the next character appeared, the chief of the state patrol, who had been having a leisurely haircut, requiring Mr. and Mrs. O.U.P. to justify their presence. So did the federal immigration officer. The workers in Roslyn are about 80-percent Slav: it is not difficult to pin on them a sufficient number of felonies to bring them under the jurisdiction of this officer also, even though they may be American citizens. The extent of intimidation was becoming clear to Mr. and Mrs. O.U.P., and the extent of illegality began to be plain with the discovery that their motor car had been searched in their absence. None the less they declined to leave without their guest. Thus the afternoon wore on till, about 5:30 P. M., there arrived the prosecuting attorney, to whom they had again to justify their presence. About an hour later Cayton reappeared and we left, the attorney giving us a short address to the effect that we had better not come back. The chief of the state patrol refused to return certain personal items to Cayton.

Cayton himself looked relieved as we left. He had spent most of the afternoon in the local jail, in a cell adjoining a black hole, whose description recalled that by Charles Reade of English prisons a century or more ago. Being prudent as well as courageous, he had concealed a few blankets in the black hole, in anticipation of being locked in there later, and had snatched some sleep on the others. His examination had been stupid and severe, including an ominous looking-over by a couple of Vigilantes, and his final release, no charge being established, was accompanied by the threat that next time he would be "handed over to the Vigilantes. Remember Yakima." It was at Yakima that the Vigilantes beat up an organizer, cutting a swastika on his scalp and "U.S.S.R." on his back. There is little likelihood of the workers forgetting that. The O.U.P. began to understand his relief and to realize that if he and Mrs. O.U.P. had not remained, the lad—he is about twenty-four—would certainly not have emerged undamaged and, being a Negro, would have been lucky to emerge alive.

What is behind all this can perhaps be explained by quoting three conversations, as nearly as possible verbatim.

One: Scene, office of the Chief of Police. Present, Cayton and chorus of police, Vigilantes. "You—You're the— ." (I am afraid the editor will cut this scene so we'll go to scene two.)

Two: Lounge of the Travelers' Hotel, headquarters of the state patrol.

O.U.P.: "Now, why is the situation so tense?"

Chief of State Patrol: "Well, it's not the men so much as the women. They use such foul language. The British sailor is said to use the foul-est language (a gratuitous insult at which the O.U.P. is too startled to protest), but these women are beyond anything you have ever heard. And we won't stand for that."

Mrs. O.U.P.: (naively): "Is it necessary to use tear gas to stop them?

C.S.P.: "Well. . ."

Three: Scene the same.

Prosecuting Attorney: "May I ask a few questions?"

O.U.P.: "By what right? So far neither I nor my friend has been accused of anything."

P.A. "Well, you see, when you're administering martial law, or near martial law, you have to do things. . . ."

O.U.P.: "You either have martial law or you don't. Has it been proclaimed?"

P.A.: "No, but it probably will be. These people are in a dangerous mood."

And the moral of that is—what? To the O.U.P. three things seem clear. First, that fascism, which to Easterners with whom he spoke seemed merely a possible danger impending in the realm of federal government, is here in the West a present fact. It operates through intimidation and illegality. It is "boring from within" by getting control of a variety of local situations. This will prepare the way for control of national situations.

Second, the movement does not like to be observed. Whatever the po-lice may have failed to do, they at least succeeded in preventing the O.U.P. from obtaining any first-hand information. The local chief of police professed utter ignorance of what the trouble was all about—a falsehood too obvious to deceive even an O.U.P. and one reflecting seriously on the chief's competence both as a policeman and as a prevaricator. He should have thought up something better.

Third, America's present troubles are not signs of economic difficulties but of moral turpitude. The Roslyn women swear; and Vigilantes, seventy-two state patrolmen working twenty hours per day at a daily cost of around $5 to $6 per man, cannot stop them. The O.U.P. guesses that the real trouble in Imperial Valley is solely that the Mexicans, the sons-of-bitches, insist on spitting into the ir-rigation ditches.

E.M. Hugh-Jones.

benefits. His decision that an election was not warranted was contained in an order that was binding until 20 October 1934.

The W.M.A. refused to accept this decision and maintained its strike. Picketers engaged in some rock and egg throwing, and even some beatings occurred of U.M.W.A. miners who crossed W.M.A. picket lines. U.M.W.A. loyalists had the full support of the Northwest Improvement Company, as well as that of the state police, whose use of power in Roslyn and Cle Elum was criticized as illegal in an article that appeared on 30 May 1934 in the *New Republic*, a nationally distributed opinion magazine.

Whether the threat to public safety was severe enough to call in six dozen state police is difficult to judge from available evidence. This amount of police power appears to be out of proportion to the gravity of the incidents recalled by Roslyn residents who at the time took opposite sides in the conflict. On one day, according to Charles

Rushton, the picketers amounted to "a gang of women and kids." And Clyde Fischer recalled that at the Number 5 mine "the women took the sheriff of the county, and took him down and one woman put her bare hind end in his face, rubbed it it his face—a dirty thing like that happened."

The futility of protracting the conflict into the summer quickly became evident in the face of the combined strength of the U.M.W.A. and company, supported as they were by federal, state, and local governments. Charles Rushton recalled that many people had to leave town for good, because the company would not hire them back. The U.M.W.A. locals contributed to selective rehiring by drawing up lists of men who were identified as "okay" or "no good," and by so doing determined the fate of many miners.

According to George Gasparich, whose father had joined the W.M.A., this rehiring process caused much bitterness that lasted

Smoke rises from the boiler house of the N.W.I. Number 7 mine in Cle Elum.
Photograph courtesy of the Roslyn Museum.

Low clouds hang over the valley facing the N.W.I. Number 5 mine between Roslyn and Cle Elum.
Photograph courtesy of the Washington State Historical Society. Photo by Asahel Curtis.

Loaded and unloaded mine trips pass at the entrance to the N.W.I. Number 5 mine in 1929.
Photograph courtesy of the Washington State Historical Society. Photo by Asahel Curtis.

for years and sparked periodic fights in area taverns. Clyde Fischer remembered that of "half the men that worked here, the old men, lost their jobs. They [the company] got rid of all the old men, that was just the ideal deal. Then they had all new young people. Old deadheads, you know, thence they got rid of their pension and everything just that easy. They just got rid of them. There is some fellas right now that went on this strike and they lived and died here and they never had nothing, only what they'd saved. It was a sad thing."[10]

CHAPTER 9

The End of an Era

By most economic measurements, Cle Elum and Roslyn endured a period of sustained decline during the quarter century from 1935 to 1960. Each of the area's three economic mainstays—coal, forest products, and agriculture—underwent profound transformations during these years, with one result common to all three: reduced opportunities for employment or livelihood. As a result, Roslyn and Cle Elum declined in population, as displaced workers moved on and as more and more graduating high school students decided to seek their fortunes elsewhere.

Farmers were first to feel the effects of changing conditions after World War I, and the hard times that ensued extended beyond the twenties into the Great Depression. The smaller scale of upper valley farms made them generally less competitive after World War II, except in certain specialized niches or as a part-time activity. This reality contrasted sharply with the aspirations of early pioneer settlers in the valley and with the initial commercial successes of the pre–World War I years.

The depression came early to farmers after World War I, not only in Kittitas County but throughout the nation as well. During the teens farm commodity prices had risen steadily, and along with them farm income. These were years when it seemed that almost anyone could earn his living on a farm. In 1919, however, prices for agricultural products began to drop, and in the space of just a few years lost one third of their former value. Land values declined sharply as well, ruining many farmers who had contracted to buy property based on its 1918 valuation.

For most of the 1920s, farm profitabilty remained marginal at best. Only toward the end of the decade, in 1927 and 1928, did rising crop prices once again begin to justify optimism for farmers. But the collapse of Wall Street and the almost total economic depression that followed wiped out the meager gains of the late twenties for most

A Labor Day parade in 1917 brings a crowd to Cle Elum's Pennsylvania Avenue (on facing page).
Photograph courtesy of Albert Schober.

A tractor, automobile, and horses team up to bring in the hay on this Kittitas County farm.
Photograph courtesy of the Museum of History & Industry.

farmers and reduced many to subsistence living. Certain traditional cash crops, such as hay that commanded $20 per ton in 1920, sold in the mid thirties for only $5 per ton. Wheat that had sold for $2.75 per bushel during its World War I peak dropped to 38

A threshing machine fills sacks with grain at harvest time.
Photograph courtesy of the Museum of History & Industry.

cents per bushel in 1932. Some farm prices dropped so low that farmers could not even recover their shipping costs.

Although the farm crisis was national in scope, the specific effects on farm communities varied from one locality to another. In all parts of the country the changing farm picture favored the survival of larger farms and ranches to the detriment of smaller operations. In Kittitas County this meant that, in the future, most agricultural activity would center on livestock raising, particularly on the larger ranches of the lower valley.

Although some small farmers in the upper valley would continue to find local outlets for hay and other crops, the area's dairymen were for the most part fated to extinction. As time passed it became increasingly difficult to compete with larger and more distant rivals as capital-intensive mechanization made local businesses like the Cle Elum Creamery, founded in 1911, uneconomical. Although World War II again rescued farmers by bringing sharply higher prices, in the postwar period increasing utilization of bulk processing and mass distribution networks reduced most small farmers to the status of marginal producers.

The end of World War II also marked a turning point for the forest products industry in Kittitas County. In the first place, the end of the wartime economy and the return to civilian life of thousands of young veterans created an unprecedented demand for housing. In the second place, the heirs of the Cascade Lumber Company's original stockholders sold out to a new management group that soon launched an ambitious modernization program of the company's Yakima mill.

But the logging industry that produced lumber and plywood to rebuild the nation's housing stock during the fifties and beyond had changed dramatically from the prewar

A Fourth of July race in 1914 brings out young and old alike in Cle Elum.
Photograph courtesy of Albert Schober.

Every girl on this gaily decorated float in Cle Elum felt like a princess on 4 July 1908.
Photograph courtesy of Albert Schober.

era. Chain saws and hydraulically operated loaders both sped the work in the forest and reduced the size and costs of manpower. Roads replaced rails, and allowed a reduced number of loggers to live in towns and commute daily to most forest worksites. Although bad for lovers of tradition and romance, these changes benefited a timber industry that remained one of the few bright spots in the local economy during the postwar period.

Commercial control of the forests in Kittitas County during the sixties, seventies, and eighties has remained the nearly exclusive domain of two large corporations. One of these is the Boise Cascade Corporation, which was formed in 1958 through the merger of the Cascade Lumber Company and the Boise Payette Lumber Company. Its Kittitas County operations are managed from Ellensburg with a district office in Cle Elum. The other major forest products company in the region, Plum Creek Timber Company, is a Seattle-based subsidiary of Burlington Northern Inc. The company maintains a "forest resources management unit" in Roslyn and operates a wood chip plant constructed near Cle Elum in 1967–68.

For most of the first half of the twentieth

A deserted Burlington Northern depot maintains a vigil over the Cle Elum yard, now primarily a storage spot for empties.
Photo by the author.

If flags measured patriotism, the Cle Elum spirit would be matchless.
Photograph courtesy of Albert Schober.

century, the Northern Pacific Railway's Land Department pursued a policy of selling land with timber on it. This practice ended around 1940, and in subsequent years the Northern Pacific contracted to sell timber only. Late in the 1950s, however, after completing an inventory of its forest resources, the Northern Pacific concluded that it could increase its annual timber harvest from approximately five to ten million board feet to forty or fifty million board feet, and still only cut at a rate that about matched the amount of new growth for the year. This "classic" form of sustained yield forest management was pursued by the Northern Pacific Railway and then by its successor company, the Burlington Northern Railroad, for approximately two decades.

Then, around 1980, changes in management personnel prompted a new look at the business practices of Burlington Northern Inc. The corporation was restructured so that divisions began to be treated as distinct businesses. Thus the railroad, the timberland group, the real estate operation, etc., each became separately accountable for returning a profit on its assets and investments. The consequence for BN Timberlands—which Burlington Northern renamed Plum Creek Timber Company in 1983 after acquiring a forest products company of this name—was to increase its annual harvest of merchantable timber from the forty to fifty million board feet pace of the sixties and seventies to approximately one hundred million board feet during the eighties.

One of the objects of the faster cutting rate was to lower the average age of the trees on Plum Creek's timberlands. Since trees grow fastest during their first fifty to seventy years, it is relatively less efficient to leave uncut stands of timber that contain a high number of one hundred year old trees. This increased rate of cutting has been coupled

Northern Pacific coal cars line up to be loaded at Cle Elum during the 1950s.
Photograph courtesy of the Roslyn Museum.

with a reforestation program that Plum Creek forestry planners believe will result in the growth of new stands of merchantable trees in as few as fifty years. Through innovative practices, such as refrigerating seedlings for several months before transplanting them to the cold slopes of the eastern Cascades, Plum Creek has increased its seedling survival rate and now replants with fewer trees per acre than before.

The Death of King Coal

Following the conclusion of labor troubles in Kittitas County in 1934, the coal industry looked brighter than it had for many years past. A steady decline in annual production of coal finally ended in 1933, and 1934 actually showed a slight increase in tonnage. Eight more years of nearly constant recovery gave the Washington coal industry a final hurrah.

During this period of relative optimism, both the N.W.I. and the privately owned Roslyn Cascade Coal Company built new facilities and modernized some old ones. In 1935, for instance, the N.W.I. replaced the large old employee wash house at Roslyn with a smaller one, and constructed a modern coal cleaning plant near the Number 5 mine. At this plant, coal cars dumped unwashed coal into a pit below the tracks. The coal was then brought up to the plant by conveyor, washed, and reloaded into the waiting cars at a rate of 150 tons per hour. New facilities were also completed at the Number 9 mine. Roslyn Cascade followed a year later with construction of a new tipple, railroad yard, automatic washing facility, and coal dryer at its site west of Ronald.

But despite the new investments and the somewhat stronger coal markets of the mid

A Northern Pacific switch engine performs yard duty in Cle Elum.
Photograph courtesy of Albert Schober.

to late thirties, the outlook for the Washington coal industry remained troubled. For one thing, the increase in production that began in 1933 followed a steep decline in output of more than fifty percent in Kittitas County from 1927 to 1933, so that any recovery started from a much lower base. A second problem was the development during the thirties of the diesel electric railroad locomotive. Although the Northern Pacific did not place its first units into service until the late 1940s, the progressive dieselization of the railroad's motive power during the fifties caused a further significant drop in railroad demand for Kittitas County coal.

Unlike the experience of World War I, the entry of the United States into World War II did not result in a rapid increase in demand for coal. In fact, total Washington production dropped significantly during 1943, and

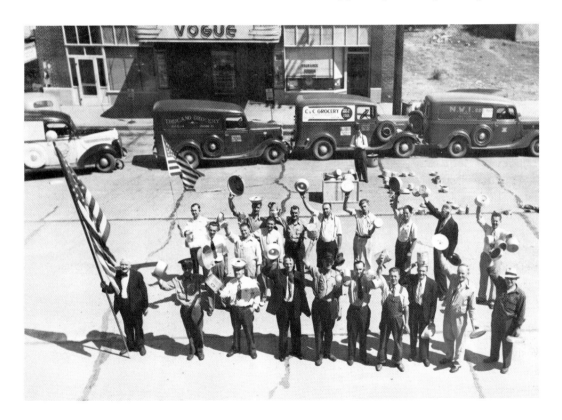

A World War II scrap iron drive yielded dozens of pots and pans.
Photograph courtesy of Albert Schober.

after a near flat performance in 1944, continued to decline in 1945. Clearly the trend in the United States was to replace coal with alternative forms of energy, particularly oil, and in the Northwest, to increase the use of hydroelectricity.

The postwar years from 1945 to 1963 witnessed the final throes of a dying industry. The largest percentage decrease during this period came early, when Kittitas County production dropped thirty-two percent from 1945 to 1946. After two years of modest recovery, coal production resumed its inexorable decline. During these last few years mine operators persisted in hoping for the best, and continued both to experiment with and to install such new labor saving devices as the Joy "continuous miner." At the same time they employed stripping methods to salvage coal that lay too close to the surface to be safely mined by underground methods.

Until close to the bitter end, operators continued to look for cheaper and safer methods of extracting coal. In his report covering development work, the state coal mining inspector reported on a new hydraulic mining method being tested in late 1961 at the Northern Pacific's Number 9 mine. Unlike much automated mining equipment, this device was suitable to steeply dipping coal beds such as those found in the Roslyn field. The tests showed that a single nozzled apparatus could increase production to twenty tons per man-shift, compared to twelve to fourteen tons by conventional methods. And the use of a multinozzled apparatus promised to double these results.

The end to commercial production in Kittitas County came in 1963. Of the dozens of coal companies that had operated in the Roslyn field, only two survived to the finish. These were the N.W.I. mines, which operated during the last five years as the Coal Division of the Northern Pacific

Railway, and the Roslyn Cascade Coal Company. The industry died not for lack of coal, but for lack of sufficient demand at a price that would fully cover costs and return a profit.

A Glimmer of Hope

In retrospect it is clear that coal mining in Kittitas County might not have ended as soon as it did. Hopes for a new future for the coal industry were born in 1952 when a group of citizens formed the Kittitas Valley Development Association for the purpose of promoting a coal fired steam plant at the

mine mouth. C. E. Miller of the Miller Lumber Company in Cle Elum spearheaded the group which was comprised of prominent representatives of local business and industry from Roslyn to Ellensburg.

As a result of the group's efforts, the proposal to construct a coal fired steam generating plant near Lake Cle Elum received serious attention during the mid fifties, when analyses of future load re-

The Cle Elum City Band was organized in 1902.
Photograph courtesy of Albert Schober.

The Cle Elum Eagles Drill Team posed for this photograph in 1932.
Photograph courtesy of Albert Schober.

White shoes distinguish the gals from the guys on the Cle Elum High School Band of 1954.
Photograph courtesy of Albert Schober.

quirements indicated a need for additional electricity in the early 1960s. By 1956 the State Power Commission had prepared a plan to build and operate the plant. In a news account from 19 December 1956 the *Seattle Times* reported that the N.W.I. was interested in selling its mining equipment and leasing its property to the state for the purpose.

During the next two years the idea was studied further, and by October 1958 a Seattle consulting engineer declared that it was feasible to build a 250,000 kilowatt plant. In the meantime politics had killed the State Power Commission, and responsibility for contracting for future power generation had passed to local utility districts or combinations of utility districts.

As a result, the Kittitas County Public Utility District assumed a leading role in studying the Cle Elum steam plant. The 1958 report was particularly encouraging, for it showed that the cost of producing electricity would compare favorably with nonfederal hydroelectric facilities then under consideration, and that sufficient coal remained to fire one plant for one hundred years or two for fifty years.

By June 1961, as Roslyn prepared to celebrate its seventy-fifth anniversary, the *Northern Kittitas County Tribune* reported that "immediate hope of a revival of the once great Roslyn coal industry rests in a coal-fired electricity generating plant, proposed by Ernie Miller of Cle Elum, advocated by the Kittitas County Development Association and backed by all Upper County organizations including the Roslyn Kiwanis Club and Upper County Miners' Unions."

These hopes were soon dashed. After Congress barred federal development of electric generating facilities at Hanford in 1961, an effort was launched to build the Hanford generating plant under the auspices of a cooperative public agency known as the Washington Public Power Supply System. The key element in this proposal was utilization of an existing Hanford nuclear reactor that produced waste steam as part of its cooling process. Gaining approval of this controversial plan taxed the political abilities of Senator Henry M. Jackson, one of the project's leading supporters.

At times the Hanford project appeared doomed, however, and new life was breathed into the proposed Cle Elum facility, the state's only ready alternative. This occurred in mid 1962 when news of a setback to the Hanford generating plant caused the Kittitas and Grant County public utility districts to begin drawing up plant specifications and negotiating power contracts. On 27 July 1962 the *Seattle Times* reported that construction would cost $90 million and employ one thousand construction workers for a period of three years. Operating the facility would provide jobs to as many as five hundred men in the plant and mine.

In the end, of course, the Washington Public Power Supply System did surmount all the regulatory and political hurdles that

threatened to block development of the Hanford generating plant. Because this thermal plant used inexpensive waste steam, its cost to the utilities was far lower than the proposed Cle Elum facility. This "bottom line" consideration, more than any other factor, stopped the Cle Elum project in its tracks and led to the final abandonment of coal mining in Roslyn.

For many years following the near go-ahead for the Cle Elum coal plant, electric

The Roslyn Eagles Band, Aerie 696, is shown installed on the steps of the Roslyn City Hall.
Photograph courtesy of the Roslyn Museum.

utility planners kept this resource in mind as a standby solution to power shortages in the Pacific Northwest. But at every critical juncture, when utilities had to decide how to meet new generating demands, lower-cost alternatives were found. In the late 1960s, for example, Northwest public utilities needed to acquire new generating capacity to meet power commitments made to California under the terms of an intertie agreement. The Cle Elum prospect again came under study, but was abandoned when two private utilities found plentiful coal near Centralia that could be strip mined at much lower cost.

Other plans to market the area's energy resources have proved to be just as ephemeral. Such was the announcement by California Time Petroleum in February 1971 that it had leased 6,400 acres of coal field from the Burlington Northern, and hoped to sell two million tons of coal per year to Japan. A *Seattle Times* story announcing the deal optimistically reported that work on a new shaft to the Number 9 mine would start "this year." Two years later, following the evaporation of plans to reopen the mines, the same newspaper reported that Roslyn, with a population of around 1,200, was "slowly dying now."

The 1947 Cle Elum semipro baseball team poses before a pile of coal waste.
Photograph courtesy of Albert Schober.

A festive occasion brings a band to the front of Cle Elum's Central Hotel around 1910.
Photograph courtesy of Albert Schober.

The seventies will long be remembered as the decade of O.P.E.C., when the price of petroleum soared and alternative sources of energy finally became commercially feasible. In retrospect this decade will probably have made a greater impact upon the manufacturers of woodstoves and the woodsmen who scavenge, chop, and distribute cordwood than to those corporations and individuals who still hope to cash in on Kittitas County coal reserves. Still, plans occasionally surfaced, such as in 1979 when the United States Department of Energy discussed the potential for "gasification" of Roslyn coal.

There is no question that plenty of coal remains in the Roslyn coal field. Geologists estimate that of total deposits of 345 million tons, only about eighteen percent, or 63 million tons, has been mined to date. How soon or whether this energy resource will again be tapped probably depends upon the costs of alternate fuels, since with present technology Roslyn coal is more expensive to mine than most other western coal.

Coal miners' shoes in the Roslyn Museum offer silent testimony to days gone by.
Photo by the author.

CHAPTER 10

Shaping the Future

During the past one hundred years, the residents of Roslyn and Cle Elum have both shaped and been shaped by history. From the sturdy pioneers and the first coal miners of the 1880s to chip mill operators and restaurateurs of the present day, individual residents have determined the ways in which they and their neighbors will live, work, and play in a community. As individuals they have made choices and voiced opinions; as a collective body they have united for their common good and to help neighbors in need.

The wider world has also impinged upon Roslyn and Cle Elum, however. The timing of the valley's settlement by United States citizens, the marketability of its mineral and forest resources, and its position as a relay station in a heavily traveled transportation corridor are important factors for understanding how and why Roslyn and Cle Elum developed as they did. As a result, these two cities' destinies were shaped at various times during the past by policies made elsewhere—often hundreds or thousands of miles away—by individuals who measured the quality of their decisions in terms of objectives and priorities not always shared by local residents. In a significant way—by surviving in the face of adversity—Cle Elum and Roslyn have met the challenges that accompany change.

There are reasons to believe that the future bodes well for Cle Elum and Roslyn, even though the communities' former major in-

dustry may never again contribute significantly to the area's prosperity. The basis for this judgment is an appreciation of the present importance and future potential of tourism and recreation in upper Kittitas County.

Cle Elum has long functioned as a relay station for travelers. From the time Walter Reed laid out the town and enticed the Northern Pacific depot to his site, local merchants and innkeepers have catered to the needs of workers and travelers away from home. The level of need for services has varied in recent decades, especially as businessmen felt the effects of the discontinuation of logging camps, the elimination of railroad traffic, and the construction of the interstate highway bypass.

Some residents of Cle Elum have welcomed and even promoted changes in the way their community attended to travelers' needs. The number of taverns in the city is only about one-third of its historic high, and the houses of prostitution that once lined Railroad Street are now gone. The brothels closed around 1960, during Mike Rossetti's first term as mayor, when a group of citizens challenged the city's toleration policy. Following a vote on the matter by the city council, the operators were given one week to shut down.

At present Cle Elum's tourist traffic comes principally from three sources. Truck drivers en route to or from Puget Sound destinations favor Cle Elum as a low-cost resting

Memorial Day in Roslyn is a day of remembrance—of servicemen, family, and friends (1985 photo on facing page).
Photo by Connie Coleman.

Roslyn High School is shown in this photograph under construction in 1909.
Photograph courtesy of the Roslyn Museum.

businesspeople with temporary worksites in the upper valley area. A third source is the traditional tourist who has made the upper valley a recreation destination and uses Cle Elum as a vacation headquarters.

During the last decade tourism has become increasingly important to Cle Elum. The number, variety, and quality of restaurants has increased, and new kinds of facilities, such as the "bed and breakfast" inn, have emerged. Cle Elum also offers a central shopping and business district that is unmatched in the rest of the upper valley. In this era of easy highway travel, a single supermarket serves residents, tourists, and inhabitants of smaller communities to the north and west. And although the number of gas stations has declined (from as many as twenty in 1949 to little more than a third of that number now), Cle Elum also sells most of the gasoline purchased in the upper valley.

The tourism and recreation industries

and dining stop, and furnish some motel operators and restaurant owners with a steady flow of year-round business. Another important market for hospitality services is provided by traveling state workers and

The Roslyn Cafe building is a historic neighbor for the Roslyn Museum at the corner of Second and Pennsylvania.
Photo by the author.

have also impacted Roslyn, but in a less visible way. As early as 1961 a writer for the *Seattle Times* noted that recreation, along with logging, had "taken the place of mining as Roslyn's leading source of income." A decade later another *Seattle Times* writer suggested that Roslyn "hovered between picturesque decay and conversion to a weekend and retirement center for Seattleites."[1] It is fair to say now that Roslyn has succeeded in accommodating citizens of all ages and at the same time arresting the decay of its important stock of historic structures. (The entire built-up portion of Roslyn became a National Historic District in February 1978.)

The distinctiveness and integrity of Roslyn's frontier-style architecture attracted Hollywood director Stanley Kramer to Roslyn in the summer of 1978. For more than a month Roslyn buzzed with excitement as cameras rolled for "The Runner Stumbles," a 1920s period film. Dick Van Dyke was cast in the leading role in this mystery about a

Catholic priest accused of murdering a young nun in his parish. According to Kramer, the townspeople adjusted well to Hollywood-style demands. "We're touching everybody's toes up here and trying not to step on any," Kramer said. "The cooperation's been fantastic."[2]

But Hollywood was not first to discover

A trio of historic structures still typifies the central business district of Roslyn in 1986.
Photo by the author.

My photo,

Taken March 1st 1906,

While at work,

Age 74 years and 35 days.

Wm Van Buren,

Cle-Elum, Wash.

William Van Buren made shoes in Cle Elum around the turn of the century.
Photograph courtesy of Albert Schober.

Roslyn. For years tourist dollars funded the construction of homes near Lake Cle Elum, many occupied primarily on weekends by Seattleites. Gradually the town's restaurants and taverns enjoyed increased business, and finally Roslyn began to reverse its population decline and to arrest the dilapidation of its stock of surplus housing.

Some of the buyers of older Roslyn homes during the 1970s were young adults seeking a low-cost and less hectic lifestyle than that typically found in cities. For a time a culture clash of sorts resulted in tense relations between some of Roslyn's long-standing residents and newcomers who many considered to be "hippies." In ensuing years these relations have improved considerably, and mutual respect appears now to be the dominant sentiment.

The Roslyn City Hall and Library began its life three-fourths of a century ago as the Y.M.C.A.
Photo by the author.

Roslyn residents of every background are often united on certain issues that evoke strong expressions of sentiment. One of these issues is the protection of the Roslyn water supply. Roslyn's water comes from the small watershed of Domerie Creek. This creek originates in the hills separating Lake Kachess from Lake Cle Elum and flows southeast into the Cle Elum River just west of Roslyn. The latest round of controversy concerning the Roslyn water supply began in 1977 when the Burlington Northern announced plans to harvest timber on two sections of land it owns in the watershed.

The timber harvest plans brought more than three hundred Roslyn residents to an S.O.S. (Save Our Shed) meeting in March 1977. Leaders of this ad hoc group expressed concerns that an improved and extended road into the area would entice recreationists, increase pollution and risk of fire, and upset the basin's ecology. Burlington Northern responded in June with an engineers' study that asserted that the Roslyn water supply was inadequate for the town's needs.[3]

This attack upon the Roslyn water supply further galvanized public opinion against Burlington Northern. The gravity-fed, unfiltered municipal water system, long a source of local pride, quickly assumed symbolic importance in what Roslyn residents perceived to be a David-and-Goliath-like struggle. For two years Roslyn residents placed their hopes in a state permitting process that they believed would ensure full environmental protection. Then Roslynites learned to their horror that municipal water supplies were not covered by state law. Their response, in March 1980, was to annex the Domerie Creek watershed to the City of Roslyn and to create a municipal permitting requirement for any activity there that would affect the public interest of Roslyn. It was not the first time the Roslyn city council had jealously guarded Roslyn's access to Domerie Creek water. Nearly sixty years earlier, in 1922, city fathers had turned down a request to supply the neighboring city of Cle Elum with surplus Roslyn water.

The preemptive move by the Roslyn city council was said to have infuriated the Burlington Northern. A *Seattle Post-Intelligencer* story on 31 May 1981 reported that the corporation found its Roslyn adversaries to be stubborn and paranoid, and quoted a company spokesman as saying that it was still studying the possibility of road-building and timber harvesting in the area. At stake in the two-square-mile tract of land were stands of virgin timber worth about $2 million.

The opposition of Roslyn residents and the availability of less controversial tracts of land for timber cutting induced Burlington Northern's Plum Creek Timber Company subsidiary to shelve temporarily its Domerie Creek plans and to explore the possibility of a timberland trade with the United States Forest Service. By 1986 negotiations were continuing, although Burlington Northern says the Forest Service has shown little enthusiasm for acquiring land ownership within the Roslyn city limits.

Dirt Bikes, High Walls, and Coal Mine Openings

Another subject that provokes intense discussion in Roslyn is off-road motorcycle riding. There is hardly a permanent resident of the upper valley who will not venture an opinion, usually negative, about the manners and recklessness of dirt bikers and the noisiness of their machines. Serious proposals for doing anything about the problems the bikes create are seldom offered, probably because most Roslynites accept the fact that dirt bikes are the preferred playthings of countless weekenders and their adolescent offspring. Still, the subject serves as a rallying point for locals, one that

The Roslyn Foundry in 1978 employed Tad Riste as manager, with Tom Blair, Brandt Lee, George Abourezk and Mike Tomac.
Photograph courtesy of the Roslyn Museum. Photo by Dennis Larson.

points out a difference between year-round and seasonal residents.

The phenomenon has its serious aspects. Sociologists have studied why and how people play, and some have concluded that people's toys bear a relationship to the tools of their ancestral trade. According to this theory, it is logical that generations of residents who earned their living with mining machines and chain saws would equip their grandchildren with snowmobiles and dirt bikes.

From an entirely objective point of view, the hills above Roslyn and Cle Elum offer an almost matchless resource for dirt biking. This land, which is designated timberland under the ownership of the Burlington Northern and a few other corporations, is laced with roads and former roads built to provide access to mining and logging operations. It is also endowed with numerous excavated trenches. These generally present on one side a cliff-like face, gently rounded at the bottom, but attaining often an angle approaching ninety degrees at the top. Features such as these attract daredevil bikers who practice their skill at ascending

Roslyn's Immaculate Conception Church was built in 1887, and rebuilt after fire damage in 1932.
Photo by the author.

and descending such highwalls.

These highwalls are the physical remains of strip mining. They share the terrain with other evidence of coal mining, such as fanhouses, bunkers for storing blasting powder, foundations of other structures and copious amounts of rusted cable, empty powder cans, and the like. For visitors to the hills, a walk or ride through the woods can provide numerous distractions.

The same industrial activity that left these deposits of what archaeologists call "cultural materials" has also created some hazards, however. Highwall climbing by bikers is one example, but many more abound. Exposed openings to mineshafts sometimes hundreds of feet deep have existed for many years in the area, as well as many smaller or shallower openings into mineworkings. Because underground mining occurred close to the surface, sometimes as close as the depth of surface treeroots, coal mines have left weakened hillslopes in some places

The Roslyn branch of the Cle Elum State Bank opened in 1908 and occupied this building in 1910.
Photo by the author.

that over the course of years or decades can crack and slide downhill. The result in some cases are openings that present a hazard to careless or curious passersby.

The potential for personal injury and property damage from abandoned mine lands such as exist in the Roslyn coal field became an object of concern to the Department of the Interior's Office of Surface Mining during the early 1980s. In the previous decade the government had stiffened reclamation standards for discontinued mine operations, and also began levying a tax on operators to pay for the investigation and reclamation of hazards on abandoned mine lands. After one false start in 1982, the Office of Surface Mining commissioned a pilot study for the state of Washington that focused on the Roslyn coal field. The study specifically included abandoned mine lands on property that had *not* been mined by the Northern Pacific Railway. (The effect of this decision was that only a small portion of the

This 1947 model "Rockola" jukebox in the Roslyn Cafe still plays twenty hit tunes on 78 rpm discs—and for a nickel a play!
Photo by Connie Coleman.

coal field, generally the peripheral areas, has been intensively examined for hazards.)

The Spokane-based consulting firm hired to perform this work spent approximately six months during 1983–84 performing field work and research. Its report identified more than one hundred unreclaimed mining sites, and its recommendations led to the closure in 1985 of six or seven of the most hazardous openings. Among these was the Roslyn Cascade "Patrick mine" rock tunnel near Ronald, whose ceiling had collapsed just behind its metal-grate-covered entrance, leaving an open access to mine works that extended more than a mile and emerged on the other side of the Roslyn–Cle Elum ridge. The accessibility of this tunnel was well-known to many local residents, as confirmed by interviews conducted on numerous occasions at the Brick Tavern in Roslyn and the Old #3 Tavern in Ronald.

The reclamation work undertaken by the Office of Surface Mining has eliminated

The Roslyn Theatre serves the entire upper valley with motion picture entertainment.
Photo by the author.

This Cle Elum High School was built in 1904.
Photograph courtesy of Albert Schober.

closer to home than even homeowners have realized. The end of the active mining era around 1960 and the increase in demand for recreational property engendered a land boom in the area around Lake Cle Elum, especially during the late 1960s and the early 1970s. Landowners, some of whom were owners of former coal properties, platted subdivisions on and around areas where coal had been mined both from the surface and underground.

On both sides of state highway 903 residential lots exist among or near areas of surface land subsidence (caused by the collapse of the mine roof into the "room" where coal was extracted), around surface excavations, or astride mounds of coal waste. For the most part the mining related hazards discovered in residential areas of the Roslyn coal field were not considered severe. Still, the Office of Surface Mining did close two small openings in and near the Pinelochsun subdivision, and notified other homeowners there of the presence on their property of mine related features.

some hazards that exist in the Roslyn coal field, but certainly not all. Others that are identified in the future may still qualify for reclamation under agency supervision. [For information, contact the Office of Surface Mining, Abandoned Mine Lands program, Denver, Colorado.] In the meantime residents and visitors alike should take common sense care when hiking or biking around the Roslyn coal field.

In some instances coal mine hazards are

Prospects for Future Development
The three major components of the upper valley's local economy for many years were

Cle Elum was already a tourism service center in 1930 when this photo was taken at the junction of the Sunset and Inland Empire highways.
Photograph courtesy of the Washington State Historical Society.

mining, forest products, and tourism. Since 1962 coal has virtually ceased to contribute to the area's prosperity, except in the form of monthly pension checks for retired miners. But unless the economics of Roslyn-field coal extraction change drastically, there appears to be little chance for a return of the mining industry to Roslyn and Cle Elum. Timber related jobs will continue to sustain dozens of area families, but this activity can be cyclical, and often depends for its health upon circumstances totally beyond local control—like demand for housing and level of mortgage interest rates. Fortunately, other industries—many of them small and inconspicuous—are contributing to the economic prosperity of the Roslyn–Cle Elum area.

The single most important of these is tourism and recreation. Because it is endowed with great natural beauty and is situated in close proximity to the state's most populous region, the upper valley will continue to attract increasing numbers of visitors, vacationers, and seasonal residents. These facts provide the basis for an optimistic view of the future economic vitality of Roslyn and Cle Elum. The direction and the extent of further development of this industry will depend in part upon the leadership, vision, and daring of individual residents, and in part upon commitments taken together by the communities of Roslyn and Cle Elum. The challenge is to remain forward-looking, while understanding, appreciating, and drawing upon resources created in the past.

The welcome sign has long been out on the state highway that joins Roslyn and Ronald to the city of Cle Elum.
Photograph courtesy of the Roslyn Museum.

John C. Shideler

John C. Shideler is president of Futurepast: The History Company, a Spokane, Washington, history consulting firm. John Shideler earned a Ph.D. in history at the University of California, Berkeley, and has taught undergraduate and graduate history courses there and at other universities. His other books include *A Medieval Catalan Noble Family: The Montcadas, 1000–1230* (1983), a portion of *A View of the Falls: An Illustrated History of Spokane* (1985), and *A Century of Caring: The Sisters of Providence at Sacred Heart Medical Center, Spokane, Washington* (1986).

A Pacific Northwest native, John Shideler founded Futurepast in 1983. As a consultant to George Maddox and Associates, he came to the coal mining areas around Roslyn and Cle Elum in 1983 and 1984 to investigate the hazard potential of abandoned mine lands for the U.S. Department of Interior's Office of Surface Mining. In conducting research for his report to the Office of Surface Mining, John Shideler became intrigued by the history of Roslyn and Cle Elum and decided to write this book.

Futurepast: The History Company provides a broad array of consulting services to businesses, institutions, government agencies, and communities. With the collaboration of specialists in other social and physical sciences, Futurepast undertakes projects that focus on the preservation, interpretation, and practical use of information and resources from the past.

Notes

Notes to Chapter 1:

1 The source for the geological theory presented here is a book by David D. Alt and Donald W. Hyndman, *Roadside Geology of Washington State* (Missoula, MT: Mountain Press Publishing Company, 1984). The accompanying charts are reprinted with permission of the publisher.

2 Owen B. Toon and Steve Olson, "The Warm Earth," in *Science 85* (October 1985), pp. 50–57 (quoted material p. 55).

Notes to Chapter 2:

1 Chinook legend as told by Bill Dietrich, "Washington's Indians," part 1 in *Seattle Times* (15 December 1985), p. C 2.

2 Howard Zinn, *A People's History of the United States* (New York: Harper Colophon Books, 1980) pp. 152–53.

3 *Indian Affairs. Laws and Treaties*, vol. 2 "Treaties," ed. Charles J. Kappler (Washington, DC: U.S. Government Printing Office, 1904), p. 699.

4 *An Illustrated History of Klickitat, Yakima and Kittitas Counties* (Interstate Publishing Company, 1904; reprinted Evansville, IN: Unigraphic, Inc., 1977), p. 66.

5 Quoted by Bill Dietrich, "Washington's Indians," part 2 in *Seattle Times* (16 December 1985), p. B 4.

Notes to Chapter 3:

1 A. J. Splawn, *Ka-mi-akin: Last Hero of the Yakimas*, 3rd printing (Yakima, WA: 1958), p. 159.

2 Notes from an interview of Bat Masterson, conducted by John Deonigi, and supplied to the author by Fred Krueger.

3 *Illustrated History of Klickitat, Yakima and Kittitas Counties*, p. 247.

4 Ibid.

5 In *Spawn of Coal Dust: History of Roslyn 1886–1955* (Roslyn, WA: 1955), see for example pp. 320, 322–23, and 339.

6 Ibid., pp. 322–23.

7 *The Times Atlas of World History*, ed. Geoffrey Barraclough (Maplewood, NJ: Hammond Inc., 1978), p. 221.

8 *Illustrated History of Klickitat, Yakima and Kittitas Counties*, p. 248.

9 Story told by Robert Bell, Sr., in *Spawn of Coal Dust*, p. 183.

10 *Spawn of Coal Dust*, p. 224.

Notes to Chapter 4:

1 Mathew Josephson, *The Robber Barons* (New York: Harcourt Brace Jovanovich, 1962), p. 243.

2 See Louis Tuck Renz, *The History of the Northern Pacific Railroad* (Fairfield, WA, 1980), pp. 117–133.

3 *Spawn of Coal Dust*, p. 196.

4 *Illustrated History of Klickitat, Yakima and Kittitas Counties*, p. 249.

5 Edwin J. Saunders, *The Coal Fields of Kittitas County* (Olympia, WA: Washington Geological Survey, Bulletin No. 9, 1914), p. 17.

6 *Spawn of Coal Dust*, p. 9.

7 For sources concerning Governor Semple's intervention, including the material directly quoted in this chapter, see *Report of the Secretary of the Interior*, vol. 3 (Washington, DC: U.S. Government Printing Office, 1888), pp. 913–17.

8 See Constitution of the State of Washington, Article I, Section 24.

Notes to Chapter 5:

1 Joseph Daniels, "Mining in the Roslyn Clealum Field," in Saunders, *Coal Fields of Kittitas County*, p. 180.

Notes to Chapter 6:

1 King Mus, "Early Settlers Expected Cle Elum to be Pittsburgh of the West," in *Ellensburg Record Centennial Edition* (July 1953), p. D 5.

2 *Spawn of Coal Dust*, p. 214, which erroneously reports the year as 1886.

3 For a fuller treatment of these events than is presented here, see Frederick E. Melder, "A Study of the Washington Coal Industry with Special Reference to the Industrial Relations Problem" (Master of Arts thesis, University of Washington, 1931), esp. pp. 48–92.

4 See *Washington (state). Annual Report of the State Mine Inspector for the Year 1904* (Olympia, WA: 1905).

5 *Annual Report . . . for the Year 1907* (Olympia, WA: 1909).

6 Introduction to biennial publication of the *Annual Report . . . for the Year 1911* and the *Annual Report . . . for the Year 1912* (Olympia, WA: 1913).

7 *Annual Report . . . for the Year 1915* (Olympia, WA: 1917).

8 *Washington (state). Annual Report of Coal Mines. For the year ending December 31, 1919* (Olympia, WA: 1920).

9 Introduction to biennial publication of the *Annual Report . . . for the Year 1895* and the *Annual Report . . . for the Year 1896* (Olympia, WA: 1897).

10 *Annual Report . . . for the Year 1904* (Olympia, WA: 1905).

11 *Annual Report . . . for the Year 1907* (Olympia, WA: 1908).

12 *Annual Report . . . for the Year 1909* (Olympia, WA: 1911).

13 *Annual Report . . . for the Year 1911* (Olympia, WA: 1913).

14 Introduction to biennial publication of the *Annual Report . . . for the Year 1911* and the *Annual Report . . . for the Year 1912* (Olympia, WA: 1913).

Notes to Chapter 7:

1 "Voices of Washington: Horselogging in Washington" (Seattle: Metromedia YMCA, 1980), taperecorded comments.

2 Jack Whitnall, in "Cascade Lumber Company" (an unpublished manuscript supplied to the author).

Notes to Chapter 8:

1 Zinn, *People's History of the United States,* p. 369.

2 Melder, "Study of the Washington Coal Industry," p. 95.

3 Ibid., p. 106.

4 Ibid., p. 113–14.

5 Ibid., p. 107.

6 Ibid., p. 115

7 Jonathan Dembo, "Washington's Early Mining Organizing," in Discussion Guide 14, distributed with "Voices of Washington: Mining Disputes in Roslyn, 1934" (Seattle: Metromedia YMCA, 1980), pp. 17–19.

8 "Voices of Washington: Mining Disputes," taperecorded comments of Camilla Saivetto, secretary-treasurer of the WMA Women's Auxiliary, and Clyde Fischer.

9 Ibid.

10 Ibid.

Notes to Chapter 10:

1 *Seattle Times,* 25 June 1961 and 11 February 1971.

2 *Seattle Times,* 15 July 1978.

3 *Seattle Times,* 6 June 1978.

Acknowledgments

It is always a pleasant undertaking to thank individuals who encourage authors and facilitate their work. Many persons have contributed in some way to the preparation of this book, and it would be impossible to cite them all by name. I especially would like to thank those residents of Roslyn and Cle Elum who have greeted this project with enthusiasm and have answered my questions and responded to my calls for help.

I am pleased to acknowledge expressions of support for this book from the Roslyn Centennial Committee, chaired by Carol Kanyer and Dave Divelbiss, and from the Cle Elum Pioneer Days Committee, chaired by Monty Moore. I wish to extend special thanks to Carol Kanyer. Carol encouraged me from the moment that I broached the idea of writing this book in the spring of 1984, and graciously lent me her copy of *Spawn of Coal Dust*. I am also grateful to Fred Krueger for sharing information and teaching materials, and to Albert Schober for allowing me to partake of his experiences and for granting me permission to reproduce his photographs.

Special recognition is also due to the late Frank Musso, whose tireless dedication to the promotion of Roslyn history is widely known and appreciated. Both through his museum work and by his willingness to discuss Roslyn's past with neighbor and visitor alike, he enriched the lives of those who knew him well or who made his casual acquaintance. I am glad to have had the opportunity to meet and talk with him.

Many other people have helped with various stages of the preparation of this book. The staffs of many libraries and museums across the state of Washington were most helpful. In particular, I wish to thank Dr. Standish Mallory of the Burke Museum at the University of Washington for his help, and Mary Andlar at the Roslyn Museum for her kind assistance. I also owe a special debt of thanks to C. W. "Buzz" Walker for teaching me most of what I know about geology and coal mining, and to Al Haslebacher, whose research on the history of native Americans in the Pacific Northwest facilitated my writing of chapter two.

I am also indebted to Bruce "Utah" Philips, my good friend and neighbor, who has helped orient my thinking on a number of aspects of labor history. For research assistance I would like to thank Rosalie MacCary, and for the graphic design of the book, Doug Crabtree of Coons, Corker & Associates. Finally, I appreciate the support and understanding that my wife Olivia and my children Gregory, Stephanie, and Julia have given in the months since I began this work.

Author's Note on Sources

There are many sources for studying the history of Roslyn and Cle Elum. It has been possible to consult only a portion of them in the course of preparing this book. Newspaper accounts in the *Seattle Times* and the *Seattle Post-Intelligencer* have provided much useful information for every period in upper valley history. Another important source was the annual reports of the state coal mine inspector, published biennially by the state printer in Olympia. For Roslyn, a major source was the community history project *Spawn of Coal Dust,* published in 1955.

Because the history of Roslyn and Cle Elum is interrelated with the national history of the United States, I have consulted some general works. These include Howard Zinn's *A People's History of the United States* as well as some standard texts in American history. Because the book is intended for a general audience, I have used endnotes sparingly — generally for the purpose of identifying directly quoted material the source of which is not otherwise indicated in the text.

Primary and Secondary Sources

Other books and articles have been useful for specific chapters or themes. Some of those that are not cited in the notes are identified below. For chapter one, they include Ruth Kirk (with Richard D. Dougherty) *Exploring Washington Archaeology* (Seattle, 1978). For chapter four, I consulted Will Dawson, *The War That Was Never Fought* (Princeton, NJ, 1971), Yvonne Prater, *Snoqualmie Pass: From Indian Trail to Interstate* (Seattle, 1981), and W. D. Lyman, *History of the Yakima Valley, Washington, Comprising Yakima, Kittitas, and Benton Counties,* 2 vols. (1919). I also read some original correspondence of V. G. Bogue preserved at the Washington State Historical Association in Tacoma.

Much of the information in chapter five came from research in United States Bureau of the Census records. Microfilmed editions of the actual census records from Cle Elum, Roslyn, and Ronald were consulted, along with abstracted information from the results of the 1890 census. Finally, for chapter nine, a useful perspective on the proposed Cle Elum coal fired steam generating plant was supplied by Ken Billington, former executive director of the Washington Public Utility Districts' Association.

Photographs

Photographs reproduced in this work have come from more than a dozen sources across the state of Washington. Two major sources are the private collection of Albert Schober in Cle Elum, and the Roslyn Museum collection in Roslyn. I have also drawn from the collections of the Washington State Historical Society in Tacoma, the Yakima Nation Library in Toppenish, the Yakima Valley Museum & Historical Association in Yakima, the Museum of History and Industry in Seattle, the Burke Museum at the University of Washington, and the Special Collections Division, University of Washington Libraries.

Other photographs come from the Local History Collection of the Ellensburg Public Library, from the Northwest Collection of the Spokane Public Library, and from the private collection of Jack Whitnall in Yakima. Contemporary photographs were taken by Connie Coleman of Seattle and by the author.

Book design by Doug Crabtree.

About the Author and the Second Edition

John C. Shideler, PhD, is president of Futurepast: Inc., an Arlington, VA–based environmental management firm that provides consulting, training and auditing services to clients worldwide.

John came to the coal mining areas around Roslyn and Cle Elum in 1983 and 1984 to investigate the hazard potential of abandoned underground coal mine lands for the U.S. Department of Interior, Office of Surface Mining. In conducting research for the final report, John became intrigued by the history of Roslyn and Cle Elum and decided to write this book.

In writing *Coal Towns,* John drew upon his background as a former professor of history and author of several other history books.

John is a native of the Pacific Northwest. He earned BA and MA degrees in history from the University of Washington and a PhD degree in history from the University of California, Berkeley. Since 1990 he has made his home in the Washington, DC, area.

Futurepast specializes in helping organizations establish and maintain environmental management systems for such purposes as preventing pollution, reducing impacts from emissions of greenhouse gases, and achieving sustainable development. Futurepast's website address is www.futurepast.com.

The Second Edition of *Coal Towns in the Cascades* appears again after being out-of-print for more than ten years.

The text of the book is unchanged from the first edition, but an index has been added and the author's biography has been updated.

The second edition also has a new publisher, Futurepast: Inc., of Arlington, VA.

Index

A

Abourezk, George, 141
Ahtanum River, 19
Alaska, 6, 12
Alpine Veneer Company, 75, 79
Americans, in "Oregon," 18; settlement of Washington, 27
Allport (Pennsylvania mining engineer, first name not known), 108-109
American Federation of Labor, 118
Anderson, Archie, 43
Anderson, William, 43
Ashue, Cecilia Smith, 7
Associated Industries, 112
Astoria, 17
Austrian immigrants, 61-62

B

BN Timberlands, 129
Baker, Thornton, 35
Balboa, Vasco Nuñez de, 12
Beekman, *see* Jonesville
Belgian immigrants, 61
Ben Snipes and Company Bank, 58
Bering Strait, 6
Black Americans in Roslyn, 46-55, 61, 62
Blackfeet tribe, 12
Blair, Tom, 141
Bogue, V. G., 40, 42
Boise Cascade Corporation, 93, 128
Boise Payette Lumber Company, 128
Bostock, Clarence, 115
Botting, David, 86
Brennan, Thomas, 34
Brick Tavern, 57, 143
Brosius, C. P., 42
Brown, D. A., 79
Brown, E. K., 118-119
Buchanan, Isaiah, 43
Burlington Northern Inc., 128-129, 140-141
Burlington Northern Railroad (successor to the Northern Pacific Railway), 128-129
Busy Bee Mining and Development Company, 79, 81
Bullitt, Logan M., 43
Bunker, Lloyd, 119

Bureau of Indian Affairs, *see* United States Department of Interior, Bureau of Indian Affairs
Bush, B. F., 74

C

California Time Petroleum, 134
Canadian immigrants, 61-62
Cape Disappointment, 1
Carbon cycle, 4-5
Carpenter, Frank, 71
Cascade Lumber Company, 70, 90-91, 92, 93, 94, 95, 98-99, 126
Cascade Miner, 75
Cascade mountains, 1
Cascade range volcanoes, 3
Casland, 98-99
Cayton, Revels, 120
Cayuse tribe, 12, 15
Celilo Falls, 20, 24-25
Central Hotel, 135
"Challie Sam," (reputed founder of New York Café in Ellensburg), 37
cemetery (in Roslyn), 54, 136
Central Baths, 59
Centralia, 2, 134
channeled scablands, 7
Chicago, Milwaukee, St. Paul and Pacific Railroad, 70-72, 83
China Camp, 37
Chinese in America, 35-37, 44, 61
Chinook creation legend, 11-12
Chinook tribe, 12, 14
Clark, William, *see* Lewis, Meriwether, and William Clark
"Clealum Junction", 31
Cle Elum (also known as "Clealum"), 1-2, 30-31, 40, 42-43, 44-45, 57-75, 125, 137-138, 141; voluntary fire department, 73
Cle Elum City Band, 131
Cle Elum Coal Company, 59, 78
Cle Elum Creamery, 126
Cle Elum Eagles Drill Team, 132
Cle Elum High School, 110, 144; School Band, 132
Cle Elum Land and Development Company, 71
Cle Elum Livery and Draying, 51

Cle Elum River, 29, 59, 140
Cle Elum–Roslyn Beneficial Association Hospital, 74
Cle Elum semiprofessional baseball team, 134
Cle Elum State Bank, 71, 142
Coal Labor Board, 119
Columbia, 14
Columbia Basin, 3
Columbia River, 11-12, 14, 17, 19, 20, 24, 27, 40
Colville, 17
Colville Indian Reservation, 24
continental drift, 1
Cook, James, 12
Cooke, Jay, 39
Cortes, Hernan, 12
Cottle, Harry, 43
coulees, 7-8
Cowlitz Pass, 40
Coxey, Jacob, 59
"Coxey's Army," 58-59
Czech immigrants, 61

D

Dawes Act (1887), 24
De Smet, Jean, 16
Deonigi, John, 32
Depot Bar, 67
dirt bikes, 141
Domerie Creek, 140-141
Draeger Rescue Apparatus, 88
Drake, Francis, 13

E

Eli, Cecelia, 6
Ellensburg, 9, 28, 30, 59
English in the Pacific Northwest, 13-14, 17-18, 60, 62
Eocene epoch, 3-4

F

Falcon Hall, 75
farming, 126
Fera, Anita Baker, 35
Ferguson County (Washington Territory), 27
Ferrelo, Bartolome, 12

Ferrimond, Sam, 118-119
Finnish immigrants, 96
Fischer, Clyde, 118, 122
Fleming, Thomas, 43
Fort Simcoe, 21
French Canadians in the Pacific Northwest, 14
French capitalists, 71

G

Galler, John, 27
Gamble, Thomas, 29, 42, 44, 59, 70, 77, 78
Gasparich, George, 122
German immigrants, 61-63
Giles (pioneer farmer, first name not known), 29
gold, in Kittitas County, 71
Goldendale, 27
Graham, H. E., 43
Grant County Public Utility District, 133
Gray, Robert, 14, 17
Greek immigrants, 96

H

Hanford Nuclear Reservation, 133
Harlan, Robert, 116
Harney, William S., 16
Hawkins, S. S., 29
Hezeta, Bruno de, 13
Hicks (Lt. Col.), 48
High Line canal, 72
Hill, James J., 39
Hudson-Bay Company, 18
Hugg, Charles, 65-66
Hugg, George, 66
Hugg, Scotty, 65
Hugh-Jones, E. M., 120-21
Hungary, workers' revolution in (1919), 104

I

Ice Age, 5-6, 7
Idaho (boundary with Washington), 1
Immaculate Conception Church (Roslyn), 142
Independent Coal and Coke Company, 79, 113, 117
"Indian John," see Quititit, John

Indian (from south Asia) immigrants, 61
Indian petrogylphs, 35
Indian Wars (1855-58), 23, 27
Industrial Workers of the World, 96-97
Inland Empire Highway, 144
International Labor Defense, 120
International Seamen's Union of America, 112
Issaquah, 2
Italian immigrants, 45, 61, 62-63, 96

J

Jackson, Henry M., 133
Jefferson, Thomas, 15
Jensen, Nez "Cayuse," 29
Jesuit missionaries, 14-15
Johnson, Thomas, 30
Jonesville (also known as Beekman), 75, 79
Joseph (Nez Perce chief), 24
Joy continuous miner, 131

K

K & E mine, 79
Kah-milt-pah tribe, 19
Kamiakin, 19, 22-23, 32
Keelan and Ward mine, 78
Kingsbury, J. L., 40
Kitchen, Henry, 35
Kittitas band (of Yakima Indians), 28-29, 31, 35
Kittitas County, 32
Kittitas County Public Utility District, 132-133
Kittitas Railway and Power Company, 71
Kittitas Valley Development Association, 131-133
Kittitas Valley, 1, 27-28, 29, 33
Klickitat tribe, 12, 19
Klickitat Valley, 27
Klinquit tribe, 19
Knights of Labor, 37, 45-46, 52, 55, 80, 114
Kow-was-say-ee tribe, 19
Kramer, Stanley, 139

L

Lake Cle Elum, 9, 11, 29, 140, 144
Lake Kachess, 72, 140
Lake Missoula, 7

Lakedale, 78-79
Lee, Brandt, 141
Lee, Paul, 99
Leschi (Nisqually chief), 22
Lewis, John L., 105, 111, 113, 118, 119
Lewis, Meriwether, and William Clark, 14, 17
Li-ay-was tribe, 19
Longshoremen in Seattle, 112
Looking Glass (Nez Perce chief), 22
Lookout Mountain, 3
Loska, Albert, 46
Louisiana Purchase, 15
Ludi, Frederick, 27

M

M. C. Miller Company, 92
Manashtash Creek, 27, 43
"manifest destiny," 15-16
Maninich, George, 21
Marmes rockshelter, 7
Masterson, Bat, 28, 32
Masterson, James, 28, 33
Masterson ranch, 43
Medicine Creek, 1854 treaty with the United States, 22
Metcalfe, James B., 48
Methow River, 19
Mexican-American War, 16
Miller, C. E., 131, 133
Miller, M. C., 71
Miller Lumber Company, 131
Milwaukee Road, *see* Chicago, Milwaukee, St. Paul and Pacific Railroad
Mine explosion: of 1892, 53, 58, 74, 84; of 1909, 85
Miner-Echo, 119
Miners' Union, 52
Miocene epoch, 4
Morusick, John, 113
Mosquito Creek, 55
Mount Olivet cemetery (Roslyn), 54
Moxee City, 27

N

Naches River, 41
Naches Pass, 42

Native Americans, 6-7
Nelson Siding, 72
New Republic, 120-21
Nez Perce tribe, 12, 22
Nisqually, 17
Nootka Sound (Vancouver Island), 13
North American continental plate, 1
North Cascades microcontinent, 2-3
Northern Kittitas County Tribune, 133
Northern Pacific Railway, 28, 30, 37, 39-55, 70, 75, 81, 84, 92, 114, 120, 129, 130, 143; Cascades line, 30, 40-43; Coal Division, 131; land grant, 77; Roslyn branch line, 43
Northwest America, 13
Northwestern Improvement Company, 56, 69, 70, 74-75, 78, 79, 80, 88, 109, 117, 118-119, 122-123, 129-130
Number 1 mine (Roslyn), 102; explosion of 1892 at, 84
Number 3 mine (Ronald), 45, 47-48, 50, 52, 75, 103, 106, 115, 117
Number 4 mine (Roslyn), 85-87
Number 5 mine (Roslyn), 122-123, 129
Number 7 mine (Cle Elum), 112, 114
Number 8 mine (Roslyn), 76, 109Number 9 mine (Roslyn), 79, 130, 131, 135

O

Ochechotes tribe, 19
Okanogan highlands, 3
Okanogan microcontinent, 3
Okanogan River, 24
Old # 3 Tavern, 143
Olympic Peninsula, 7
Oregon, 15-18
Oregon City, 18
Oregon Railway & Navigation Company, 41
Oregon Territory, 18
Oregon Trail, 14
Organization of Petroleum Exporting Countries (O.P.E.C.), 135
Owen, C. F., 85
Owl Saloon, 67

P

Pacific Bar, 68

Pacific Ocean, 1
Pacific Ocean plate, 1-3
Packwood (sheriff, first name not known), 46-48
Packwood, S. T., 71
Paleocene epoch, 4
Palouse River, 7
Palouse tribe, 19
Panama Canal, 102
Patrick, Archibald S. (father), 43, 77
Patrick, Archibald S. (son), 77
Patrick mine, 143
Pasco, 40, 41
Pinelochsun, 79, 144
plate tectonics, 1
Perez, Juan, 13
Pisquouse tribe, 19
Plant, Amable F., 79
Pleistocene epoch, 4, 6
Pliocene epoch, 4
Plum Creek Timber Company, 128, 129, 141
Pohasti (chief), 28, 33
Populist Party, 58
Polk, James K. 16-18
Public Meat Market, 64
Pullman Company, effects in Washington state of 1894 Chicago strike, 59

Q

Queen mine, 79
Quinault River, 13
Quititit, John, 33; wife of, 34

R

Reade, Charles, 120
Reed, Walter, 29-31, 42, 44, 71, 77, 135
Reed, Barbara A., 44
Reed House, 31
Rees, William, 37
Reliable Auto Company, 115
Riste, Tad, 141
Robinson, George, 69
Rocky Mountains, 2, 6
Roman Catholic Church in Cle Elum, 61
Ronald, Alexander, 53, 75
Ronald, 62, 64, 67-68, 75

Roosevelt, Franklin D., 119
Roslyn, 1-2, 40, 42-43, 44-45, 57-75, 77, 120, 125, 135, 137-141; cemetery in, 64, 136; national historic district designation, 139; voluntary fire department, 73
Roslyn Bakery, 65
Roslyn Café, 138, 143
Roslyn Cascade Coal Company, 77-78, 89, 117, 129-130, 131, 143
Roslyn City Hall and Library, 140
Roslyn Eagles Band, 133
Roslyn Foundry, 141
Roslyn Fuel Company, 75, 78, 87, 88, 89, 113, 117
Roslyn High School, 110, 138
Roslyn Kiwanis Club, 133
Roslyn Museum, 138
Roslyn Theatre, 143
Ross, Alexander, 48-49
Rossetti, Mike, 137
Ruff, Bob, 118
"Runner Stumbles, The" (film), 139
Rupert, Ray, 89
Rushton, Charles, 122
Russian civil war (1918-1921), 104
Russian Orthodox Church in Cle Elum, 63
Russians in the Pacific Northwest, 12-14, 18, 61
Russo-Japanese War, 80

S

Sabilites palmetto, 5
Salmon Le Sac, 37, 71
Santiago, 13
Sasse Hotel, 33
Satus Creek, 19
"Save Our Shed" (S.O.S.), 140
Scandanavian immigrants, 62-32
Scottish immigrants, 61-62
Se-ap-cat tribe, 19
Seaton, Sr. (pioneer farmer, first name not known), 29
Seattle and Walla Walla wagon road, 30
Seattle General Strike (1919), 104-105
Semple, Eugene, 46-52
Shock, Jim, 34
Shyiks tribe, 19
Silvio Pellico Lodge, 63

Simcoe Mountains, 27
Sioux tribe, 12
Skin-pah tribe, 19
Slavic immigrants, 60-63, 96, 120
Snake River, 14
Snake tribe, 12
Snively, H. J., 48, 50
snowmobiles, 141
Snoqualmie Pass, 9
South Cle Elum, 71
Southeast Asia (animal fossil remains), 3
Spanish in America, 12-14
Spawn of Coal Dust, 32, 35, 37, 78
Splawn, A. J., 27-28, 32
Spokane, 17, 23, 40
Spokane flood, 7-8
St. John, Vern, 91
Stampede Pass, 30, 40-42, 44, 45
Stanley (illustrator, first name not known), 8
State Highway 903, 144
Stevens, Isaac, 8, 18, 22-23
Stevens Pass, 40, 42
Strait of Georgia, 18
Summit mine, 79, 81
Sunset Highway, 144
Swauk district mining laws, 37
Swauk prairie, 28-29,
Swauk River, 9, 59, 99
Swedish immigrants, 61

T

Tacoma, 40
Teanaway, 28-30, 70
Teanaway River (creek), 9, 27, 30, 90, 98-99,
Teanaway Valley, 28, 93, 97
The Dalles, 8, 14
Thompson, William, 43
Thorp, 9
Thorp, Fielding M., 27
Thrall, 9
Tomac, Mike, 141
Torino Saloon, 68
tourism, 145
Travelers' Hotel, 121

U

Union Gap, 9
Union Pacific Railroad, 58
United Kingdom of Great Britain and Ireland
(Britain), 18
United Mine Workers of America, 80, 104-106,
108, 109, 113-114, 115-116, 118-119, 120, 122
United States: citizenship for American
Indians, 24; treaties with Indian nations, 18-19,
22, 27, 32
United States Army, 22
United States Bituminous Coal Commission,
108-109, 111
United States Department of Energy, 135
United States Department of Interior: Bureau
of Indian Affairs, 20, 24; Office of Surface
Mining, 143-144
United States Forest Service, 71, 141
University of Washington, 88
Upper County Miners' Unions, 133

V

Van Buren, William, 139
Van Dyke, Dick, 139
Van Fleet, Guy, 66
Vancouver (Washington), 17, 40
Villard, Henry, 39, 40
Virden, George, 29

W

Wallace, John, 116
Walla Walla, 15, 19, 27; Treaty of, see United
States: treaties with Indian Nations
Wallula Junction, 41-42
Washington Public Power Supply System, 133
Washington State Power Commission, 132
Washington Territory, 18, 24
Welsh immigrants, 61-62

Wenatchee River, 19
Wenatshapam tribe, 19
Western Federation of Miners, 80, 114
Western Miners of America, 118-119, 120-121,
122
Western Miners' Union, *see* Western Miners of
America
Weyerhaeuser, George, 92
Whitman, Marcus, 15
Whitman Mission (Waiilatpu), 15
Whitnall, Jack, 99
Wilkeson Mine, 106
Willamette Valley, 15, 27
Wish-ham tribe, 19
Wolflin, H. M., 87
Woodfield, 12
World War I, xenophobia associated with, 64
Wright, Thomas B., 78-79
Wright mine, 79

X

Y

Yakima Indian Nation, 6-9, 11-12, 14, 28-29, 31,
32, 33, 35; Kittitas band, 33-35; 1855 treaty with
the United States, 19, 22
Yakima Indian Reservation, 7, 11, 19, 20-21, 24,
33, 35
Yakima River, 9, 19, 33, 89, 111
Yakima Roslyn Coal Company, 79
Yakima Valley, 27
Young Men's Christian Association (Y.M.C.A.),
74, 140

Z

Zentner, Fred, 66
Zentner's Cigar Store, 65-66
Zinn, Howard, 16